Beyond Words

Beyond Words
Writing Poems With Children

Third Edition

Elizabeth McKim &
Judith W. Steinbergh

Talking Stone Press, 99 Evans Road, Brookline, MA 02445

Cover photograph: ©1983 Cary Wolinsky

Layout and Design: George E. Murphy Jr.
Third edition revision: Elizabeth Resnick
Original composition: Rosemary Murphy

ACKNOWLEDGMENTS

Cavanagh, Margery: "Runes," from *The Custom of Living* (Wampeter Press), copyright ©1980 by Margery Cavanagh.

Conkling, Hilda: "The Cellar," from *Shoes of the Wind* (Stokes, Lippincott, 1922), copyright ©1949 Hilda Conkling. Reprinted by permission of the author.

Francis, Robert: "Blue Cornucopia," from *Robert Francis: Collected Poems 1936-1976*, copyright ©1974 by Robert Francis. Reprinted by permission of U. of Massachusetts Press.

Harada, Gail N.: "New Year," *Hawaii Review 8*, Fall 1978, Copyright ©1978 by Gail N. Harada.

Hughes, Langston: "I Loved My Friend," from *The Dream Keeper and Other Poems*, copyright ©1932 and renewed in 1960 by Langston Hughes. Reprinted by permission of Alfred A. Knopf, Inc.

Hughes, Langston: "Dream Variation," copyright ©1926 by Alfred A. Knopf, Inc., renewed 1954 by Langston Hughes.

Iza, Ana Maria: "Formula." Reprinted by arrangement with Scott, Foresman, and Co.

Janosco, Beatrice: "The Garden Snake." Reprinted by permission of the author.

Knight, Etheridge: "Haiku," from *The Essential Etheridge Knight*, University of Pittsburgh Press copyright ©1986.

Kumin, Maxine: "In the Root Cellar," from *House, Bridge, Foundatin, Gate*, copyright ©1971 by Maxine Kumin. Reprinted by permission of Curtis Brown Ltd. All rights reserved.

Li-Young Lee: "I Ask My Mother to Sing," copyright ©1986 Li-Young Lee, from *Rose*, BOA Editions, Ltd., Brockport, NY, 1986.

Mahone, Barbara: "What Color Is Black?" from *Sugarfields*, copyright ©1970 by Barbara Mahone.

Marcus, Morton: "Learn to be Water," copyright © by Morton Marcus. Reprinted by arrangement with *Kayak*.

McKim, Elizabeth: All poems copyright ©1992, 1983 by Elizabeth McKim. Used by permission of the author.

Miranda, Gary: "Witnessing," copyright ©1979 by the Atlantic Monthly Co. Reprinted by permission of the author and the Atlantic Monthly Co.

Moffit, John: "To Look at Anything," from *The Living Seed*, copyright ©1961, by John Moffit. Reprinted by permission of Harcourt, Brace, Javanovich, Inc.

Mohr, Howard: "How to Tell a Tornado," from *Minnesota English Journal*, (Vol. IX, No. 3, Fall 1973, p. 6) Reprinted by arrangement with Scott, Foresman and Co.

Mullen, Harryette: "Momma Sayings" by permission of the author.

Nam, Saykio, "Grandmother," copyright ©1983 by Saykio Nam. Reprinted by permission of the author.

Piercy, Marge: "Attack of the Squash People," from *The Moon is Always Female*, copyright ©1977 by Marge Piercy. Reprinted by permission of the author and Alfred A. Knopf.

Reynolds, Sarah Seabury: "In My Other Life," copyright ©1983. Reprinted by permission of the author.

Sexton, Anne: "The Fury of Overshoes," from *The Death Notebooks*, copyright ©1974 by Anne Sexton. Reprinted by permission of Houghton-Mifflin Co.

Spivack, Kathleen: "March 1st," copyright ©1951 by *The New Yorker*, Reprinted by permission of Kathleen Spivack.

Steinbergh, Judith: All poems copyright ©1992, 1983 by Judith Steinbergh. Used by permission of Judith Steinbergh.

Walker, Margaret: "Lineage," copyright © 1989 by Margaret Walker from *This is My Century, New and Collected Poems*, published by the University of Georgia Press, 1989. By permission of the author.

Waniek, Marilyn Nelson: "Herbs in the Attic" copyright ©1985 by Marilyn Nelson Waniek. Reprinted by permission of Louisiana State University Press from *Mama's Promises* by Marilyn Nelson Waniek.

Whitman, Ruth, "Stealing Forsythia," from *Blood and Milk, Poems* (October House, 1963) copyright ©1963 by Ruth Whitman. Reprinted by permission of the author.

Third Edition

Printed in the U.S.A.

Library of Congress Card Catalog Number: 82-70442
ISBN: 0-944941-14-1 (formerly 0-944941-03-6, Second Edition, 0-931694-13-2, First Addition)

To reorder *Beyond Words, Writing Poems with Children* and for a free catalogue of tapes and books published by Talking Stone Press, please write: Talking Stone Press, 99 Evans Road, Brookline, MA 02445, or phone 1-800-557-3100 or fax 617-734-3223.

ACKNOWLEDGMENTS

We are grateful to the following institutions and individuals for helping us to pursue our work:

The Artists Foundation and Cultural Education Collaborative of Massachusetts for helping to fund some of the Poetry Residencies in which we generated many of these poems.

The numerous public school systems that invited us, as poets, into the schools and supported our work.

The Brockton School System and Rita Lowenthal, who hosted Elizabeth as Poet-in-Residence for seven years and published the first limited edition of this book.

Brookline Public Schools, where Judith has been Poet-in-Residence for over ten years.

The Institute of Expressive Therapies and Integrated Arts of Lesley College and the Department of Creative Arts in Learning, where we work with teachers and graduate students to share and implement these ideas.

Our many friends, fellow poets, and teachers who have shared their ideas generously and Ruth Whitman who initiated and directed the first Poetry-in-the Schools program in Massachusetts.

A special thanks to Cary Wolinsky for his generosity in time and photographs.

Every effort has been made to contact, for permission purposes, the students and adults whose poems appear in this book. In a few cases, this has proved unsuccessful. The publisher will be glad to hear from these writers.

PHOTO CREDITS

Bauman Photography, Inc. 62.
Barbara E. Davis, 19, 20, 25, 37, 111.
Pete Main (*Christian Science Monitor*), 49.
Tom MacGuire, 18.
Jenifer Mumford, 98, photo of authors.
Gale Parker, 8, 136.
Dody Riggs 20, 110.
Mimo Robinson, 126.
Nancy Shakelton, 14, 28, 114.
M. Leo Tierney, 13
Gilian Wilhauer, 58.
Cary Wolinsky, Cover, 10, 16, 17, 27, 56, 65, 69, 71, 74, 75, 79, 85, 87, 89, 90, 97, 100, 109, 124, 133, 140.
All other photos taken by Judith Steinbergh or Elizabeth McKim

We dedicate this book to all the children with whom we have worked, whose poems are the most powerful statement of why poetry should have a place in our schools and in our lives -

and to our own children, Jenifer, Shauna, and David

and our grandchildren: Chloe, Max, Cheyenne, Cortni and Samantha and those to come.

Contents

A FOREWORD

This book is meant to help teachers and parents make poetry a part of their own and their children's lives. After working as poets in the classrooms for several years, we began to gather what we considered to be the best sources, ideas and techniques that we ourselves have used and found to be successful. The result is this introduction to poetry for children, a teaching guide which incorporates specific lessons. You may want to take the central ideas of these lessons and apply them to your own themes and interests. We have enriched what we gathered with poems written by adults and children. These poems serve as examples, and they offer a way for people to become familiar with a wide range of poetry, to hear what others have said in their poems, and to begin to feel more comfortable in what, for some, can be a difficult mode of expression.

In making poems, we participate in an exchange of learning with our children. At the basis of our philosophy is the belief that we are really not teaching anything but helping to reveal what is already there. Our workshops ask for common participation from everyone. We listen and learn from the children, as they listen and learn from us. There is no power or domination in these experiences; rather there is a spirit of exchange and sharing. In this book, our emphasis is on encouraging children to use their natural voice in expression, to feel self-confident in what they have to say, and to be willing to take risks.

Although we have shared the writing and organization of this book, we will use the first person "I" to simplify the presentation of material.

PART I
An Approach To Poetry

To think of a song or poem, you have to
think of yourself, of nature
and the things in the world, all the love and
happiness.
Then something comes into my mind. But it feels
to me like it never goes through my mind.
It just comes out of my mouth and I say it.
That's how my poems come to me.

Rena Johnson, 5th

Creeping up through my body
like honey dripping
from a pot into my brain
it slithers into my mind sinking
like a ship into the watery land of ideas.

Laura De Normandie, 5th

The Mysterious
     African
     Rino
is *Interested in reciting*
     All different kinds of

     Lengthy poems about everything
     And
     Giggles when he reads them under
      eUculiptis trees
     And
     Rhododendron bushes in the boiling
hot Days in
     Africa.

Maria Laguarda, 5th

Poetry the
Only limit of
Eloquence is your
Mind

Charlton Pettus, 5th

Poems are something else,
On paper, you see words, but
Elsewhere in the
Mind, you
See anything you want.

Marianna Gracey, 5th

Directions

Hold
it. Warm
it with your own
life. Hold
it to your ear. Listen
to its near and far
pulse, the sounds, the messages.
Find out where it was born:
the year, the time,
and who was there, and why.
Find out the nature
of its fear,
what cave or cliff or curve
of tide has touched it, tended
it, nested it.
Find out what it can
know of parents, what song
and language it was taught,
and if it has a friend,
an enemy; what stains
and bruises, marks
and cracks
distinguish it, what
surface opens to the air, what
inside-heart is hiding
there, and learn
the way it breathes
and moves, the way it feels
the wind, the way
it warms itself, the fire
it knows, and how
it moves upon
the earth.

Elizabeth McKim

Introduction:
A Rationale For Poetry

In a time of drastic budget cutting and a new emphasis on "Back to Basics," people often ask me "why poetry?" Is it just a frill, one of the niceties we can just as well do without? It has been my experience that poetry is a basic tool for communication, a tool which belongs to us all; useful because it helps us to say what we need to say in the fullest and most authentic way we know.

In the process of writing and sharing poetry, a child's interest in the mechanics and skills associated with writing increases dramatically. Children anxious to record their thoughts manage to write most eloquently and with more real commitment than children with little investment in what they have to say.

Children lacking the motor skills to write, children with perceptual problems which hinder their reading and writing, children with emotional difficulties often show improvement when involved with poetry. Time and again, I see children who are labeled "non-readers" standing up and reading what they have written or what someone else had recorded for them. I see children whose first language is not English wanting to find the new words for their poems, feeling freer to mix the music of two languages. For children whose verbal ability is already advanced, poetry can be a vehicle to further expand their gifts. I see shy children overcoming their fear and standing up to read their own poems aloud. And I see children developing as enthusiastic writers, carrying around sheaves and notebooks of their work, gaining respect from their friends on other than academic grounds, in an area where trust, risk and feeling is a large factor.

Poetry is a special way of perceiving the world. It is a weaving together of feelings and environment. Poets not only see things in great detail, but also see them on other levels. They may describe the actual behavior of an animal, but also see that behavior as human. They may talk about a broken vase, but also see that vase as a lost friend. In order to write poetry, one must be vulnerable, sensitive to sounds and rhythms both in language and in the surrounding environment.

Why share with children? Because they love to look and need to talk. Because they are relieved to find their experiences shared by others.

When I begin teaching poetry to a new class, I try to satisfy four goals. The first is to create an environment that is conducive to self-expression. I want the children to feel free to say what they need to say. I want them to be open and honest and to work out their concerns. To facilitate this, I also open up, make myself vulnerable, share my own dreams, fears and memories and read my poems. It also means providing them with ways to talk about themselves without feeling embarrassed. By introducing children to metaphor, simile and the use of persona in elementary ways, we can give them a chance to discuss their dreams, their fears, their perceptions of themselves and of those around them.

My second goal is to encourage children to use all their senses. I urge them to take time to observe things closely, think out details that reflect how they feel, and to experience objects, surroundings, and events with more than just intellect. I ask them to communicate their perceptions by making comparisons between the thing they are seeing and other things. These comparisons help the reader experience the world the way the writer does.

My third goal is to sensitize the children to words and extend their use of language. I want them to hear the natural rhythms and music in the way we speak. I want them to see what effect repetition has on our language and to delight in trying new arrangements of words and new structures for phrases. In order to encourage children to take words seriously, I try to create a trusting climate in which they can play with language and explore and extend the boundaries of their imaginations. By sharing their poems aloud, children improve their listening skills and begin to hear the difference the individual voice can make.

My fourth goal is to get children involved in the process of making a poem. By motivating children to write, we increase their incentive for more verbal expression and their investment in their own work. This results in children wanting to acquire language arts skills in a meaningful context and will also lead to a lasting relationship with language and literature. I want children to describe the way they see the world, rather than how others want them to see it. I want them to record their feelings and perceptions as they discover them, before they are classified. As this fifth grader writes:

> *I don't understand why*
> *the grass is green*
> *why the sky is blue*
> *why thoughts can't be seen.*
>
> *if I ruled the world*
> *the grass would be pink*
> *the sky would be purple*
> *You could see what you think.*
>
> *Charlton Pettus, 5th*

As a working artist, I share my experience and process with the students. I have poems of my own to share and, generally, a wide knowledge of other poets who can illustrate the focus of our workshops. The teacher, on the other hand, by virtue of her continuing presence in the classroom, can make poetry an integral part of the curriculum, as well as the ongoing life of the class

and give children the base in writing that can have a profound effect on their lives. The teacher should try to get as deep a knowledge of poetry and its processes as possible.

Where do you begin? Start with reading contemporary poetry. Browse through poetry at the library or in bookstores, borrow some poetry magazines, buy one or two anthologies. You will find poems and poets that please you. After a while, you will find your favorite poets, those you keep going back to as friends. Listen to records of poets reading their own work, and whenever possible, go to readings.

It is important that you participate in the act of writing if you are to work with the children; make yourself as vulnerable as they, so that poetry is a common endeavor in your class or at home.

To Look at Anything

To look at anything,
If you would know that thing,
You must look at it long:
To look at this green and say
'I have seen spring in these
Woods,' will not do - you must
Be the thing you see:
You must be the dark snakes of
Stems and ferny plumes of leaves,
You must enter in
To the small silences between
The leaves,
You must take your time
And touch the very peace
They issue from.

John Moffitt

Looking Beyond Words

the way we give meaning to words in poetry.

All our lives we are taught to label objects, experiences, ideas. Education is mostly a division of events into categories.

Let's consider the thing we call "table." The minute I acquire language, I substitute the sound symbol, "table" for the infant experience of table: touch, taste, smell, shape, color, and shadow. In a way, this is fortunate, because it allows me to communicate with other people, and to get things done. If I took the time to experience my surroundings the way a baby does, inspecting each object, feeling it, then putting it in my mouth, I would be a long time reaching my destination. However, I often lose the sensed experience of an object as I acquire more and more labels for the things in my world.

The word "table" has a *"denotation,"* a definition in the dictionary, useful to all of us. However, when each of us says table or reads "table," it evokes a different image in each of our minds. These are the *"connotations"* of the word "table," and these meanings are as important as the dictionary definition. When I say "table," I think of a round piece of dark oak, grooved and pocked with age, set on one pedestal, spiraling up like the fairy-tale spires of Danish churches, attached at the base to a cross, each bar carved down like a waterfall to the floor. It smells from years of crude oil soaking into the wood, bringing out electric swirls in the grain. I see my mother bent over, polishing the surface as she did in the days of her early marriage.

To my friend, "table" is the raw slab of pine in her office that serves as her desk. Clips are swallowed by its dark knots. Its edges stab at you with splinters. Your "table" might be teak, or glass with chrome legs. How can all these extremes be denoted by one word, "table." To communicate with each other, we must be specific in describing what we mean, personally, when we say the word, "table." If we want another person to visualize what we are saying, to experience something the same way we do, we have to look at it closely, describe it in detail, using all our senses and making comparisons with other objects. This is the way we give words meaning in poetry. In poetry, we separate the word or label from the object and re-experience the object.

It is important to experience the word separately from the object. How does it sound, how is it shaped? I say a word over and over until it becomes an abstract sound; other sounds follow. The words become chants, rhythms, take on an independent life.

Experience objects; become them. Experience words; absorb them. Then you can rejoin the words, and what they represent, with a deeper understanding of the shortcomings and possibilities of our language.

Motivations In Writing

There is no question that children have a rich store of material: experience, emotions, and images from which they can draw their own self-expression. Children who early in their lives are encouraged to draw from this material grow to believe in their own ideas. They become confident of what they want to say through their writing and rarely lack for subject matter. They do not always need the approval of teachers and adults to feel they have made something of worth. These children often grow to be capable and expressive writers who have established their own values about their work.

However, children may not always know the wide range of sources which provide writers with material, and they often have not learned the techniques which enable writers to express that material. By exposing children to a wide range of techniques in writing poetry and discussing in depth the sources available to us, children will broaden *what* they write about and *how* they write about it. Other stimuli which release rather than dampen children's own material are: a wide variety of accessible poems, the close inspection of physical objects, and individual curricula introduced in the classroom.

With any material introduced in the classroom, the primary concern is to present the students with something they can care about deeply and relate to their own thoughts and concerns. The desire to share this with others will usually follow. We write in our most authentic voice about those events, people, places, feelings, and dreams that move us most deeply.

SOURCES

The sources artists draw on for their material are available to everyone. These include our beginnings, our growing, dramatic changes in our lives, aging, dreams, fantasies, fears, joys, conflicts, relationships, places ingrained in our minds, smells that recall a past event or place, separation, death, the continuous search for who we are, our ancestors, our children, and what we observe in the world around us. In other words, all of our experience in the world is material for creative work.

As teachers we can make these sources explicit by addressing them directly one by one, bringing in material related to each, creating discussion around them and giving children a chance to express how these areas relate to their own lives.

TECHNIQUES

Exposing children to a wide variety of techniques for writing poetry and showing children many styles of poetry will dispel early stereotypes of what a poem is. This will give children a range of tools for their expression. Technique cannot be taught in the absence of content, but I want to mention a few examples, all of which would be associated with some content important to the child. Some techniques I feel are important to introduce to young children are the use of simile, metaphor, persona, repetition, parallel structure, poems of address, naming, concrete poems, and sound poems.

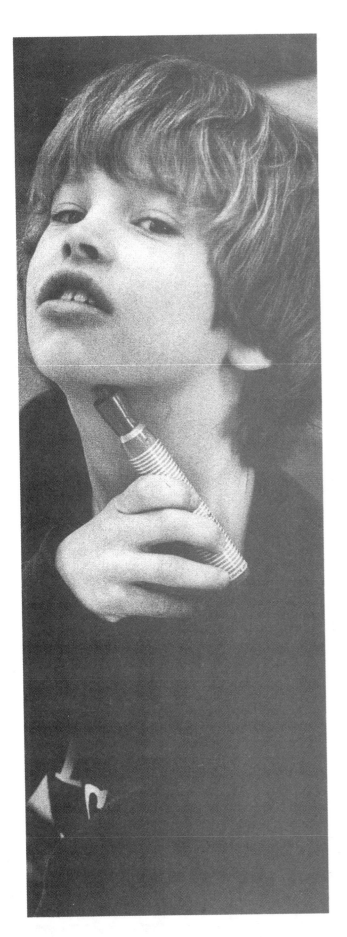

PRESENCE OF A PHYSICAL OBJECT

A painted box, a sea shell, an old key can evoke imaginative and descriptive imagery that mere discussion of the same objects will fail to generate. Video tapes of sessions where children are handling an object show how intensely their relationship with their object develops and later how it is reflected in their writing.

The children and I both bring in, collect, or discover our own favorite objects, and it is through writing with these objects that they develop skills of observation, description, imagery. Through using their senses, they come closer to the reality of an object. Encouraging children to see is Jacqueline Jackson's message in *TURN NOT PALE BELOVED SNAIL*. She says:

"The thing that will help our writing most, as well as our souls, is to begin to take time . . . . to become real watchers. To look again and again and again until what we see is soaked in and is there. Forever. To recognize that our eyes have been asleep, and start awakening them."

LITERATURE

There is nothing that can replace reading children good literature. By reading the best poems accessible to children, and by telling and reading stories, fairy tales, myths, legends and fables, we begin to develop in children a body of literature and styles from which they can draw as they continue to write. These works not only transmit content of interest, but introduce classic structures and forms which students can incorporate into their own repertoire. Later, the student may even use the form of a myth to express his own experience or idea. Or a student may choose a legend to exemplify her own personal experience. As students begin to see structures and types of characters reappearing in literature over the centuries and in many different cultures, the universal archetypes and symbols will naturally come up in their own writing. Again, the emphasis is on expanding the number of choices available for expressing personal experience.

CURRICULUM

The classroom curriculum, both formal and informal, can offer rich materials for writing. If children are learning about space or oceans or dinosaurs or mealworms, for example, expressive writing and drawing not only enriches the learning experience, but also gives children a chance to personalize the material. This greatly increases their chances of retaining it. Study of other cultures—Eskimo, Native American, African, Chinese —offer vast opportunities for reading their literature and history and absorbing the oral tradition and points of view from a different cultural perspective. Trips to museums, natural environments, musical, artistic, and dance events can all provide many new writing experiences.

If poetry is valued and validated within the daily life of the group, this expression can be a useful tool to understand not only areas and themes of academic interest, but also moments of celebration, humor, loss, conflict, compassion and anger when they arise.

FINDING A BALANCE

Finding a balance between providing "stimuli" and themes and structures for writing, and encouraging the children to find their own sources and thematic material is important. Often, as the writing process progresses and children gain confidence and begin to take pride and pleasure in their words, they also take the initiative for perpetuating their own writing. However, once the writing energy within the group has been generated, directions can be open enough to provide the space for structure as well as individual growth and expression.

Working With Students

TIME REQUIREMENTS

The timing of workshops demands some thought in order to experience a full writing process. I do not like to rush or pressure the students because they need preparation for writing: the asking of questions, the gathering of information, the focusing on theme, the experiencing of a verbal or non-verbal process to enable them to feel and internalize whatever it is they are preparing to write. Then they need solitary time for writing, and lastly, they need time at the end for sharing. I feel it is necessary to have this ending as it provides a psychological and emotional closure for feelings which arise and gives students a feeling of pride and accomplishment in what they have written.

Of course it is not always possible to devote a full hour or more to writing, and it is sometimes valuable to spend shorter, more intense moments in between longer sessions to provide a time where feelings and thoughts can be written in journals. Something may happen within the classroom experience which may lead into an unexpected poetry session such as a fight, a question, a celebration, a loss, a letter, etc. This is all part of the gathering of material, part of poetry and poem makers.

Many people worry about how to begin, how to introduce poetry to a group. I always start in a circle, usually sitting on the floor so we can all see each other. We start by sharing some poems which I have brought in, exploring together what a poem is: poems have shapes on the page and

music and rhythm when we hear them read out-loud, poems show our feelings as well as our thoughts, poems can be virtually about anything as long as we care enough about the subject to write about it. I show them poems by published poets, poems from out of the oral tradition in other cultures, and of course poems by children their age, sometimes written on large pieces of un-lined paper, words which find their way among and between shapes and colors, and in and out of drawings. These poems are by children who come to their own integral forms, often as disciplined as a sonnet or a sestina.

FORMAT OF A POETRY SESSION

I begin a class by briefly reviewing what we will do and why. For example, "I have brought in some stones and we will look at them, share together what they look like, write poems about them, and then read the poems out loud."

I present the material, reveal the objects, initiate a movement or dramatic exercise, tell a story, start the children drawing, or verbally introduce a theme. Through participation in this "warmup" we generate ideas, enthusiasm, a real impatience to begin writing.

I read some examples by children and adults. I give out paper, markers, and crayons and the children begin.

If children have a clear idea of some different thing about which they'd like to write or if they wish to continue working on writing already be-

gun, I allow it, unless I've prepared an exercise which I think the child would find particularly useful. Then I ask him to try that exercise before continuing with the other work.

Some children have difficulty beginning to write. This becomes less of a problem when they become more comfortable with poetry as a medium. Often the teacher or I will sit with these children and talk with them about the material. I may review some of the ideas which came up in the class discussion, or I may simply remind a student to start with all the things a seashell looks like and then go on to what it feels like and so forth. The following conversation is typical of what I encounter and how I handle it.

"I don't know what to write. I can't do this."

"Would you like to write about a baby whale, a mother whale, a teenage whale or something else?"

"A baby lost from its mother."

"How did it get lost?"

"It swam inside a cave when the others weren't looking."

"Does it ever get found?"

"The mother calls for it underwater in her song."

"Why don't you begin writing about this and check with me if you get stuck."

Acceptance and encouragement are essential for the growth of young writers. All children and adults, those who find writing easy and those who find it hard, will be unwilling to take new risks unless their first attempts find acceptance. At the same time, it is important to begin to instill in young writers a set of standards and values against which they can measure their own writing. Students who are always looking to adults for approval can not work effectively on their own. Early on, we must encourage them to trust their own reactions to what they like and dislike.

"I've got this so far. Is it good?"

"Do you like it?"

"I don't know."

"Well, think about it. Because it matters how you feel about your writing. I think you can go further. You didn't say anything about what the

*light is like down here or if you swim through
swells over and over again. Is it cold? Do you have
some ideas about these things?"*

In these brief one-to-one conferences with a
teacher or another   student, children can move
more deeply into their writing process.

I am engaged in helping children to express
what they think and feel. I encourage them to
articulate their experience, even if this experience
might be difficult for them, involving conflict,
anger, pain, loss, separation, sexuality, violence,
etc. I let the children give me the signals as to
how far they wish to go, to what extent they wish
to express their feelings in words. I try not to im-
pose my value system on them. However, I do
realize, as teacher-poet, that I do have expecta-
tions, restrictions and limitations for their
writing. If a child has written something which
might humiliate a classmate or embarrass himself,
or something which I view as cruel, sexist or
racist, I will talk to the child privately. (One of
the reasons adults stop writing is because long ago
a teacher *openly* humiliated them.)   I explain
why I do not wish this particular poem to be

shared with the others. It is essential to realize
that we are involved in a process which can help
us toward greater freedom and *also* enhance our
feeling of responsibility toward others.

Most of the children are now writing. I
generally leave about fifteen minutes for this part
of the session. This may seem like an extremely
short period of time, but I've found that about
two-thirds of the children will be finished within
this limit. The others can go on writing while we
begin to read. Sometimes a child can't write
during the session at all. I tell this child to draw
or make some notes for a poem and work on it
that night. It would be wrong to assume that
everyone works in the same way; it's just that
hundreds of sessions like these have shown that
many students, when excited by the material
presented, are ready to try out some writing on
the spot and often produce more when writing
in the group, feeling that group energy, than they
might have at home alone. I have known other
children who store up the ideas and integrate
them later into their writing. This is just as
valuable, perhaps more so.

I try to save the last ten minutes for reading
the children's work out loud. We gather in a circle

whenever possible, usually on the floor, and I bring my tape recorder which I have found to be an indispensible tool in my work. After the first session, the children are used to it, and I find that students who are often too shy to read to the group will read into the tape or read to the tape recorder when the others have finished and returned to their desks. The tapes provide documentation of my work and I play them for other teachers and students as well as for the original class.

I ask who wants to begin. Normally, about five children are vying to be first. In younger grades (1-4) this is always the case. By fifth grade, you may have to ask someone to begin. If I go around the circle, most everyone will read. Sometimes during the first two or three sessions, there is some resistance. A few students will ask me to read, which I will do after everyone who is reading his own has finished. However, I discourage this on the basis that often I mess up the poem by reading it all wrong and only the poet can do it justice. Sometimes they switch poems to read out loud, but this often ends in a jolty unsatisfactory reading. The children figure that out themselves. If a child has written something

intensely personal, or does not yet feel trust in the classmates or in me, he may want to keep it private. I agree and offer to look at it alone if he likes.

Listening to a poem, I tell the children, demands the same kind of care and attention that writing the poem asks. In listening, we can appreciate the voice of the poet, and the special music of the spoken word, surrounded by its silences.

As each child reads, I listen carefully for some image or sound or combination of words which is particularly exciting or successful in the poem. I try to respond honestly and with full sensitivity. I encourage the others to let the writer know what they are feeling and thinking.

"I love the way you use all those soft sounds together for your snake," or *"Those two words - cranberry dawn - are terrific. Don't you like them?"* or *"That's a great comparison between the shell and the spiral staircase."*

I try to teach children what is effective in poetry by pointing out what is working well, what moves me so that others can hear it and perhaps try it themselves. I have found this to be an effective and positive way of teaching writing

and often results in students loving poetry sessions, respecting their own writing, accepting what they have to say as humans, and trusting the teachers enough to make themselves vulnerable.

When a child is ready for criticism, she will let you know this. This kind of feed-back can be given in a casual conference in private.

When possible, I end by telling them how proud I am of their work and the seriousness with which they write. I may suggest ways they can go on with a particular technique or subject at home. "Now that we have listened to whale songs, try listening to birds outside your home in the early morning, drawing the shape of what they sing, and writing a translation of their words." Or, "If you liked my shells and bark, collect some of your own and write a short poem about each item you collect." Thus, the children take the tools we offer into their own lives.

REVIEW

Let me review once again, the steps from beginning to end:

—Review format and focus of the lesson.
—Talk about the goal of the lesson (e.g. use of comparisons, persona, parallel structure, recalling early memories, special places, fears, etc.)
—Present the material or stimuli (objects, film, record, photos, idea or new area for discussion.)
—Give clear instructions for writing.
—Read some examples by adults and other children.
—Help the children begin. Help them find ideas or help them write them down.
—Give encouragement to children to go further in their writing.
—Read poems out loud, in a circle if possible. Give positive comments when appropriate.
—Explain how the lesson can be extended outside the classroom.
—Save or display the poem.

This is not meant to be an inflexible structure which others should adopt without variation. It is a sequence which feels comfortable to me and to my teaching style. It covers the aspects of a writing workshop which I think are essential to building enthusiasm and trust regarding poetry and other kinds of writing. It gives children a chance to be exposed to new material, to talk, to listen to others' poems, to write their own and share out loud. From the school's point of view it includes listening, communication, writing and reading skills.

In addition, it offers the children a way to develop their emotional, expressive and social beings, as well as their analytical sides. It gives them confidence, pleasure, and intimacy.

First graders dancing with Judy to the poem "Way Down in the Music" by Eloise Greenfield from her book Honey, I Love.

A poem gets to me like a rainbow reaches to a pot of gold.
Like friends join hands. Like teachers and adults get to little kids.
Like fingers get to food. Like the sun sets and rises in all different colors of red, orange, yellow, green, blue and purple.
Like an apple reaches to a mouth and into people's teeth.
Like sunshine goes behind clouds. Like grass sprouts.
Like flowers bloom and blossom.
Like a bud would flutter to the ground and smell so fresh.
Like a walk through the woods with the leaves falling onto the grass with fresh morning dew all over the trees and grass.
Like love has a special touch to hearts.
Like your heart melts to love when your pets or relatives or friends die.
How the whole world joins hands because of love.
Like rain and snow fall, like the alphabet gets in order.
Like my pencil, paper, heart, hands, mind, brain and smartness from all the teachers teaching me, join together and write a poem.
Angela Warren, 5th

ORAL LANGUAGE

Sometimes, when working with young children, we chant and sing words, do movements and sounds and words in rhythm, listen to poems, tell stories together, or share orally our dreams and wishes. We share memories of when we were very small, or what our special places are, or the biggest boast we know. Listening to the tape afterward gives immense pleasure to the children and enhances their feeling toward poetry, its structure, sounds, repetitions, and special ways of feeling.

SOME MADE–UP SONGS BY KINDER-GARTENERS

Leslie
Takes a lovely leap
What does she see?
you tell me
you tell me
She sees a lovely lamb
It goes
  Baa, baa, baa,

by Leslie Collins

Mark
In the dark
Wants some milk
Meets a mouse
Mark
Dark
Milk
Mouse

by Mark Murphy

Sarah's swaying
Swaying
Swaying
Sarah's swaying
In the wind

by Sarah Petty

Sarah
Flying
Take care
Just think
Don't blink

by Sarah Whittemore

Where does
    Nicole go
When the
    ghost blows
She hides in
    the closet
Under the
    clothes

by Nicole Ritchay

Sam's in the night
Dark
Black
Turn on the light

by Sam Varela

DICTATION

Taking dictation for children in kindergarten and first grade is a crucial aspect of my work with poetry. I feel the natural rhythms of children's spoken language is often lost when they are beginning to write. The sheer effort it takes to write each word is often a barrier to expression. My goal is to have children writing their own material. But by dictating frequently in kindergarten and first grade, the children's first writing will tend to be closer to their speech instead of stilted or formal or limited to "first grade vocabulary." By balancing times when children write on their own with times they can dictate, they will continue to have the opportunity to record longer and more intricate thoughts. The need or desire to dictate some work may continue into second and, occasionally, third grade, depending on the child.

ORAL TRADITION

The oral tradition is deep, rich, wide, and far reaching. It includes the language passed down from generation to generation within a family and within a culture. It is personal: thus it belongs to the person. It becomes her. It reflects him. It circles us. It is our songs, stories, and signs. It is our myths and our messages, our lovesongs and lullabies, our boasts and our ballads, our prayers. It begins where we begin, and it is informed by our sense of place: valley or mountain, country or city. There were poems before there were printing presses. There were poems inside children before they went to school and learned to write them down. There are poems which are sung or chanted or danced, poems which tell histories of a culture, and poems which tell of suffering and oppression, celebration and joy. Teachers have the opportunity to honor the legacy of language, the words and wonderings and questions of children said in their own authentic voices, holding the power and the wonder of the spoken word. This, as I see it, is the *Bridge* which we can walk on to pass over into *Reading and Writing*. It should begin the first day a child enters school and be carried on, with enthusiasm and joy through all the years to come. It is the antidote we have against cliché, ready made words, and all the babbles, from TV babble to educo/babble to psycho/babble to politico/babble. And yes, it can bring us all pleasure.

I'm a whisker on a cat, maybe a
dimple on a chin, a tadpole swimming
in the quiet lakes and marshes,
I am a flower blooming in the big fields,
I am a rainbow vanishing.
I am a sad teddy bear. I am a flee
on a cat and a dog. It's a forest out here.
I sprinkle sand in the night in your eyes
and on the beach floor and my name is
sand man, my name is the sand man. Do
you believe in me? If you don't I won't be free.
I am a soft white deer in the meadows.

Astrid Levis-Thorne's poem written with
standard spelling and punctuation, grade 1.

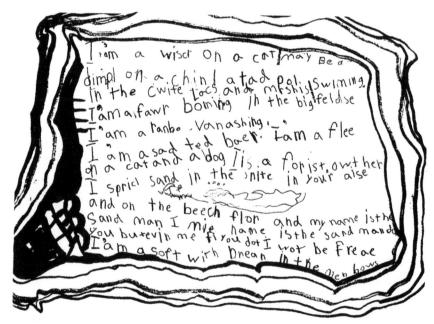

Poem by first grader, Astrid Levis-Thorne, using invented spelling.

The following poem was dictated by a boy to a teacher in the spring of first grade. He could write adequately by himself, but was sometimes frustrated by his inability to write as fast as he envisioned his poetry.

The Flying Cheetah

The wings of the cheetah-
If you do see one
Your eyes will turn magic
So you can see far beyond the universe
And across the oceans
And up in the sky
You can see the wings of the cheetah.

And if you try to catch him
He will fly away in his run
And if you saw him before
And tried to catch him again
Your eyes will turn to blood.
And the cheetah will stare at your eyes
And they will turn black like his.

Tom Moscovitch, 2nd

(This afterword was also dictated by Tom):

The author of "The Flying Cheetah" was Tom Moscovitch. "The Flying Cheetah" was an ancient poem. The poem was made into two stanzas with seven lines and with the help of Mr. Nicol. This might happen to you. Nobody knows. And this was my first poem.

In second grade, the power of Tom's language emerged in his own handwriting.

Eagle

Eagle leaps off her nest
in search of food.
Her soft wings
slide across the slippery sky.
Her sharp claws

pierce out like kitten's paws.
Eagle sees a river. Like planes land,
she swoops down onto the moving glass.
Her sharp claws
close on a fish
that wiggles like a worm.
Her strong wings flap and
like a glider,
she lifts into the air.

When children write their own material, I suggest they use the space of the page in ways that please them. They might weave their words in and around visual shapes. I offer this when I take dictation and always ask the children where on the page they would like me to write their words. They almost always feel strongly about this.

In kindergarten or a first grade, where many children are still dictating, the presence of extra hands can be very helpful. Teachers have handled this by scheduling aides, if possible, one or two parent volunteers, or older children in the school (6–8th graders) to be available when writing is taking place.

INVENTED SPELLING

The writing children do on their own will be closer to the "spoken word" if we give them the freedom and approval to use invented spelling. Children who feel safe using invented spelling write freely and often consider themselves writers very early on, sometimes before they learn to read. Studies have shown that children in first and second grade using invented spelling are not hampered in learning traditional spelling simultaneously.

The following poems were written by first and second graders who may not have risked trying such big words as motorcycle, careful, dangerous, or reflection, if they did not feel safe inventing the spelling of these words.

The Circus

I em a motsukl ridr
it is ckiree but it is fun
my and Don ar riding
wy ar korfl
but it is dajris but fun
I like to doo it

I am a motorcycle rider
it is scary but it is fun
me and Don are riding
we are careful
but it is dangerous but fun
I like to do it.

Jonathan Zagaren, 2nd

my rock is gold
and ruf and in it is
fire and sparcs but it
is smol but it is pritea
big for a rock an there is
fire on the whol but it
is not hot.

Donald, 2nd

The Sky and the Sea

The sky is
beautiful at
sunset and
the sea is
beautiful on
the refleshun
The sky has certind
things in it licke
birds and bees
and the sea has
fish and wels and
seals and lots
of other things.

David Steinbergh, 1st grade

Sometimes older children who have trouble spelling are discouraged from writing by pressures to write only what is spelled correctly. When these children are encouraged to continue their invented spellings and given help in their re-visions, we find them to be as prolific, if not more so, than the accomplished spellers.

Cheada

The cheada
an over gron cat
purrrrr purrrrr
Hids in the tall
grass, stocks his pray:
zeber, antalop and
carabe, by his self.
spots like frekls,
Hids in trees,
sits in trees,
lays in trees.

Eric Smith, 4th

SHARING THE WORK

Now what is done with the poems? Often the children put them in their writing folders or special poetry folder to be saved for a hand made book at the end of the term. If the children have journals, they may have written a draft of the poem in the journal. Sometimes we put the poems up in the room right away. Or we may want to do a lesson on revision and use the revised copies in a display on the walls, perhaps with associated visual art work.

I try to have my students save their poems in a central place so that they will have a body of work. They begin to see themselves as people who write, who make poems.

At the end of an extended series of poetry workshops, I try to gather one or two poems from each child for a class anthology. This is a gratifying process for the children, because they can look over their work and decide which poems they like best. I find having the children revise and copy their own poems on a ditto master and decorate their own page with art work makes the book even more personal and graphically exciting. This takes about two lessons to complete, as it is often a painstaking business for a child to to copy poems without mistakes onto a ditto master. Because the children know that many others will read their work, they are motivated to make sure the poem is perfect in its mechanics as well as its content.

Poems can be submitted to a school paper if there is one, and to children's magazines if the teachers and children are so inclined. Sometimes the values of these national magazines do not coincide with the values I am trying to instill in my young writers, and I do not want them to lose confidence if their poems are not accepted for publication.

Sharing the children's poems with children in another classroom or in an assembly also shows that you take their work seriously. They gain the poise and confidence to speak before an audience and can see the immediate response an audience gives when listening to a reader. Readings for parents, or in public, have often changed a child who was excruciatingly shy into a confident reader. For weeks one girl said she couldn't do it. She said she'd faint, mumble, stop breathing. I said I'd hold her hand. I wanted people to hear that fantastic poem about loneliness. I made a decision to persist with this child who would always resist sharing in public if she could not get over it in one terrifying moment. She did it. She said it wasn't bad. In fact, it was good. As a teacher, you sometimes take these risks, push a child beyond what she thinks she can do at the risk of alienating her. But you have to have her trust first and be sensitive to her limitations. You can tell stories about how terrified you've been before audiences to show her she is not alone in her fear.

The loud-speaker can be another useful device for listening to a few poems at the end of a day, and the children and teachers in the school become interested and excited about *who* is going to read *which* poem.

Poems can be combined with music, drama, or movement. Sometimes I bring in an assortment of home-made percussion instruments and have the children read their poems using one of these. Sometimes each child chooses a friend to play a musical background for the poem. Children have tried pianos, violins, recorders, guitars. In addition, I encourage children who are musical to try writing songs and these are always taped at the beginning of the next session.

Dramatizing original poems is a very effective way of sharing within a class. Groups of four or five children may choose one of their poems to dramatize. It rarely takes them more than ten or fifteen minutes to work out their improvisations. One person may read while the others dramatize it. Or children may take on different voices in the poem.

Folk musician Vance Gilbert plays along with children's poems and improvised songs.

Poem of Tall and Small

Tall: I'm tall.
Small: I'm small.
Tall: I can squash you.
Small: But I can duck under a table.
Tall: I'm as tall as a redwood tree.
Small: I'm as small as a Pepsi bottle.
Small: If there was no small there could be no tall.
Tall: If there was no tall there would be no small.
Tall: If you're tall you get the rain first.
Small: Lightning would strike tall first.
Small: The bigger you are the harder you fall.
Tall: I can dunk in basketball.
Tall: I will be seen by an oncoming truck.
Small: A lumber jack could mistake you for a tree.
Tall: You'll look like a rat if you get caught in a trap.
Small: Face it, small is better!
Tall: Short people have no reason to live.
Small: Oh yeah
Tall: Oh yeah.

Matthew Barzun, 5th

REVISION

After four or five poetry writing sessions with a class (in third grade and up), I find it is useful to talk about revision. Poetry, or any inspired writing, seems to happen most successfully in two stages. The first step is putting your thoughts and feelings down on paper with a burst of energy, disregarding spelling, grammar, punctuation, and handwriting. As a teacher, you should not let this panic you. Often the writer begins a poem or story and has no idea where it will end up. The surprises, the turns of language and event, even the mistakes are often what make the poem successful. We would not censor at this step. As writers, we need to be open and receptive and prolific. We should write more than we need to. Later we can hone and edit.

In the second step, the writer goes on to review the poem, to see if the words, images, and line breaks are the right ones, to change what needs to be changed, and to either type the poem or rewrite it with some concern for its readability. Otherwise, the poet can't share the poem with a reader. The children's eagerness to share their poems in a written form is a wonderful incentive to check spelling, really examine words and punctuation, and to rewrite as legibly as possible. The mechanics of writing cannot be ignored, but attaching them to meaningful material is one of the most successful ways of teaching them.

I bring in my first and successive drafts of a poem to show children how revision is carried out.

Not everything needs to be revised. Practicing writers constantly write yet perhaps revise only twenty five percent of their work. The rest is tucked away and possibly used at a later date. Sometimes mistakes in writing and drawing can be recycled into the finished product. A spelling or word choice error frequently surprises us with a new meaning for the poem. Some poems are given to us almost perfectly. We need to recognize when the muse is sitting on a child's shoulder. When the moment is inspired, the work should be left alone. For younger children, kindergarten to third grade, the sheer effort needed for rewriting makes me feel that they should not be required to revise more than one out of four or five poems. For third graders and older, revision can take place in short conferences with an adult or peer.

Steinbergh leading a criticism workshop with a group of sixth graders.

From fourth or fifth grade on up, students will find the chance to revise less burdensome. Prior to an event such as a reading, or the printing of an anthology, it is important to spend time revising and rewriting.

Another forum for revision is the workshop setting. Here a piece or several short pieces of work by one child are looked at carefully by a group of students and a teacher. Each workshop member has a copy of the piece which is read out loud by the author. Comments are made on the work as a whole and suggestions offered as to how the poems might be improved. All suggestions may or may not be taken by the author. We focus on the content and impact of the poem, saving the last five minutes for spelling and punctuation corrections. The student whose work is being reviewed is asked to write a revision. I always preface these workshops by saying how normal it is to feel defensive about your own poems which seem so close to you. You, as the author, should make the ultimate decision whether to change words, images, or lines. Spending a whole class period on one or two pieces of writing, not only benefits the author, but also gives the other workshop participants experience in looking closely at a piece of literature, trusting their own reactions, feeling confident enough to offer an opinion, and gaining insight into how to improve their own writing.

Snow drifting down
like salt from its shaker,
flakes sail in the sky
like white stars in the dark night.
Children play fort
like little privates in the army,
or little angels in the snow.
V's of birds
fly rapidly through the air,
trees
dancing in the sun,
branches sway left and right,
icicles drip silver drops,
a white blanket covers the ground -
it gleams in the sun,
Warm fires in fireplaces,
families cuddled in blankets
listening to stories of winter,
the night the snow falls
carolers sing carols.

Neil's first draft is written as a paragraph, a common format for students' first drafts. His second draft appears above.

Phases of the Moon

Full

A baby with a maroon balloon slowly
unclenched his fist and gently, swiftly
magically the balloon floated up. Silvery stars
clung to the balloon as higher and higher it rose
until it landed softly to rest in the sky
on an invisible bed.

Quarter

An emerald pea-pod, a smile of gratitude,
A fresh golden unpeeled banana, a crisp
crunchy melon rind, an Eskimo kayak
with the sky as its raging waters.
The arched back of an old man when
suddenly, the man is gone...

Half

The letter C, a juicy slice of cantaloupe.
Who will be the first to eat this
refreshing baby orange citrus fruit?
Everybody dig in! Each bite
tastes sort of bland, creamy, invisible.
Each bite floats
from ruby red lips to come together
like a puzzle in the sky.

New

The Queen of Fantasy and Ambition wished
to acquire all the most rare jewels of
the world; her servants searched
high and low to gather each and everyone
of the rarest of jewels.
The moon was mistaken for a golden
necklace but when the fault is realized,
it will be replaced.

Rachel Solar, 5th

A poem is magic because it can transform one thing into another.

PART II

Ideas For Writing Poems

Organization of Material

The following chapter covers sessions I think are important to poetry and to the process and craft of writing. You may be able to take off in a new direction from these or create a new idea altogether. By listening to and learning from your students, interests may emerge that become material for new poems. You may want to focus a session around your own experience, a child's special love for bugs, music, or baseball. You can invent ways to transform your enthusiasm into new ideas for poems.

However, sometimes sessions flop. They might work well with one class and not another. You need to take risks at times. I have had startling results from a class when I least expected them. As always, be sensitive to the class dynamic and be ready to revise the approach to the material when the children seem to be headed in a different direction.

What Is Poetry?

How do you introduce poetry to your class? You may have an approach with which you feel comfortable. Here are some of my thoughts.

I begin by talking a few minutes about poems. I ask them what they think a poem speaks about. Feelings and emotions. What are some of these? Imagination and fantasy? What kinds of things do we imagine? Dreams and day-dreams. Can we remember what these are. A poem deals with every day life: waking up, a fight on the playground, playing hopscotch, making a new friend, missing a person we love, feeling lonely, getting muddy, car racing, being sick in bed. A poem is about the way we interact with the rest of the world through our senses of sight, hearing, feeling, taste, and smell or about the interior world of our mind.

I say a poem is magic because it can transform one thing into another: a garden into a snake, the moon into a sail-boat spinnaker, a frog into a person. We can learn to work this magic by using simile and metaphor.

The Garden Hose

In the gray evening
I see a long green serpent
With its tail in the dahlias.

It lies in loops across the grass
and drinks softly at the faucet.

I can hear it swallow.

                    Beatrice Janosco

We talk about how poems sound. Some have a strong rhythm, almost music. Some poems are lyrical or smooth, some jagged, some like chants. If we look closely, we find words that sound alike or almost alike hidden inside the poem.

Schools of Fish

flicker
foil banners
flapping in wind

lifting
like leaves
in a twister

hover
of fluttering fins
still as whispers

glittering gems
in a ring
flute stream/riverfall

breath of a comet
sparks in a liquid night
moon tipped wing

vortex of light

                    Judith Steinbergh

O See On Prism Poem for Boomer

how i wish
silver fish

how bout you
fish in the stew

hushaby swimmer
slide and glimmer

see-saw
jelly daw

fish see me
i see he

ooo oo
bubble me too

oceanic
rag yeah blues

Elizabeth McKim

There are many ways of structuring a poem. The use of rhyme is one of them. Repetition and parallel structure are others. Syllabic poetry is yet another. It is important for children to be exposed to all the poetic techniques so they may get as close to their authentic voice as possible. For young children, the flow of expression is easier if they don't always have to be concerned with formal structure. Poems have as much to do with content and sincerity as they do with form.

It can be simple to make a friend
if you can make it.
I couldn't.
I tried everything, but I couldn't
Then I showed him my strength.
       The end.

Nate Herzog, 1st

Finally, I ask them what a poem looks like. This is a hard question because some poems (called prose-poems) don't look much different than prose. However, most poems have shorter lines than prose. The language of poetry is often concise or condensed.

The shapes that poems have are deeply connected to the meaning of the poem and the voice of the poet. For example, if a poet wants to convey elements of movement such as flowing or hesitating, moving with nervous jerky motions, or leaping, she can reveal it in the shape of the lines and space on the page.

Rolling
grass
  hair
   sky
    ground
     silence
     sound
      hold your breath
      faster
     down
      green
       blue
        watch out
       bumping
       blue
        green
         nothing's what
          my eyes are shut
       faster
       faster
        don't want
        to stop
         do you?

Judith Steinbergh

Some poems have special forms that require the line or stanza to be a certain length. Some poems end their lines at the ends of phrases or sentences or at the ends of important words.

Poem

I loved my friend.
He went away from me.
There is nothing more to say.
The poem ends,
Soft as it began - -
I loved my friend.

Langston Hughes

My Tongue

Why are you so long? So you can sing
me a song? Why are you so wide and
wavy like the tide? The good ti-
mes were when I was little and
I got into a fight and I th-
ought it was right to st-
ick my tongue out at all
my friends, that I did
not like. I like to li-
ck the bowl filled wi-
th pudding and lick
the jar and try
to reach for a
star to ca--
tch snow
flakes
as they
fall.
My,
tongue!
You
know
your
way
around!
Shelley Kruskall, 7th grade

I give out large sheets of unlined drawing paper. Many of my students have unlined hard-bound or spiral-bound sketch books. The poems can be inside a simple shape or around it. Poems about water might be written in waves. Poems about milk-weed seeds might have words floating up and over the meadow. I continually reinforce the idea of the page as a space to explore, not necessarily having to start the poem at the top left side. This choosing of where on the page to begin gives children a sense of how closely the visual and verbal arts are related, and also gives children who are more comfortable in the visual modes the freedom to use this expression.

How a poem is written on the page corresponds to the sound and silence of a spoken poem. Therefore, where the poet pauses, hesitates or comes to a full stop corresponds to where one breaks a line. Writing a poem is a little bit like notating music and demands listening to the voice of the poem. Encourage the children to read their poems aloud and listen to where the pauses come. Take a poem by a contemporary poet (e.e. cummings would be good for this one) and have the children listen and write the poem on the page the way they hear it.

Of course there will always be some children who write from one margin to the other without fail, no matter what you do. In this case, it is best to let go any rigid definitions of what poetry looks like. Concentrate on the expressed feelings, authenticity of expression and qualities of imagery. Return to and reinforce, as time allows, the many shapes and possible arrangements of words and lines of the page, and how these groupings of words correspond to the spoken voice.

Ways to Begin — Word Games

WAYS TO BEGIN — WORD GAMES

In the beginning, it is important to find ways of introducing children to poetry so they do not feel threatened by failure. The following is an exercise which introduces children to writing poetry through a sense of play.

WORD BOWL

The "Wordbowl" is a beginning exercise in poetry which helps children break out of their traditional approach toward language. It makes magic of words, and provides an alternative to cliché or the oppression of the blank page.

An important element in beginning poetry is play; that's why poets generally have a lot in common with children and take them seriously. (I don't just *want* to play, I *need* to play.) Experimenting with words, finding images and word combinations which can startle or delight or move me in some way, is part of the work, the play.

If I put something in a totally new environment (for instance, "my mother inside a twice-lit candle" or "tomorrow sitting in silence with its hands on its knees") my imagination *may* begin to work, and in time I may write a poem. And even if I don't, I have handled the *stuff* of poetry, the material, just as a painter handles paints, or a potter handles clay.

It is often these curious combinations and conjunctions of words which startle the writer into the poem. Also the very fact of manipulating the words, discarding some, trading others, adding what one needs for sense, can teach us something about selection and choice in making poems. We can see that a poem *looks* different from a story; it has its own shape. We can handle the words and make new lines and phrases, change these lines and see how the content changes with the form. Using two or three words together that normally don't appear together can make fresh images, charging them with new energy and excitement.

How do you begin? With your children, find a bowl: salad, copper, glass, or even an old cooking pot. Then sit down for some time with some poetry books, novels, cookbooks, and anything else that strikes your fancy. I've always preferred poetry books because the words are so rich, but nature, nursery rhymes, science, geography or almost any field of human interest can and should be used. Then just make combinations, phrases or single words, free associating as much as you want. Make sure you have plenty of connectives, pronouns, verbs, nouns, prepositional phrases, etc. Make the words and phrases as lively, colorful, and amusing as possible.

After you have your list, making sure you have a wide and wondrous selection, take some scissors and cut off each word or phrase and put it in the bowl. As you go along, you can keep adding words, choosing words from books, or

magazines, using children's own words out of their own personal experiences and knowledge or out of a classroom experience.

On the following pages are some of the words I found. You can photocopy and cut these up and begin to add your own words.

(Photocopy these words and phrases to begin your Word Bowl.)

GRASSES
WHISTLES
PIRATE
HONOR THYSELF
TERRIBLE
JUNKYARD
BONES
RABBIT TRACKS
HANDS
LACY FERN
BOULDER
TISSUE
GRIN
IN CLOVER
THUMP
RIPPLES
HISS
BUZZ
RUMBLE
RATTLE
SHAKE
RUSTLE
LEAVING FOREVER
JUNGLE
TEMPLES
CRISS-CROSS
MARBLES
HOPSCOTCH
JUMP ROPE
NUTS
UNDIVIDED
STRAWBERRY
MIDNIGHT SUN
SUNFLOWER
CLOSES
SUPERMAN
CHICKEN LITTLE
GIANT
HEAT
BITTERSWEET
CRASH
BUMP
DART
ZOOM

AMBLE	CITY CATS	SAND DUNE
HONK	HOLLER	I WILL
BEEP	WATCHES	YOU AND I
STOREFRONT	BROWN	CREEPY
CHURCH	HANGS OUT	SHIMMER
FIRE	AROUND	DANCING
WAITING	BEHIND	TRUST ME
LONG LINES	BLACK	RED ORANGE
LOTTERY TICKETS	BETWEEN	BLUE SILVER
BIG MUSEUM	CONCRETE	MAGENTA
YELLOW	BACK STEPS	LILAC
SKIP	OVER	LOPING
SISTERS	JAZZ	DARKNESS
KEYS	HOMEGIRL	HOOTING
MAMA	SLOW BLUES	OILY
BIG SHINY CAR	SWEEP	GIDDY
ARGUE	MY COUSINS	GLAZED
DISCUSS	ALIVE	NUZZLED
EBONY	IVORY	WHIR
APPRECIATE	IN THE	COBBLED STREET
HOMEBOY	MARKET	GARBAGE
RESPECT	AUNTIE	STREET LIGHT
SUMMERTIME	BUTCHER	NEON
ANSWER ME	FLOWERPOTS	TRAFFIC
THE PANIC OF	HYDRANT	STOP LIGHT
ZIP	SPLASHING	SIREN
ASUNDER	ALLEY	CROWDED
EGG	JUICY	WATCH OUT!
BREATHING	PITS	DOUBLE DECKER
EAGLES	BOUNCE	FRONT PORCH
KITES	BALLOONMAN	AT THE COURTS
CANARY	TREE TRUNK	PASSING
PRAIRIE	SHADE	DUNKING
TANGERINE	ACORNS	GIRLS JUMPING
FLOATING	DRIFTWOOD	DOUBLE DUTCH
SWAYING	REFLECTIONS	SWINGS
HAYSTACK	SMOKE	SEE-SAW
BRIDGE	LEOPARD	TOUCH TAG
PUDDLE	PEPPER	RAP
SPINACH	DIMPLES	HIP HOP
STOP	JOLLY	GRAFFITI
DUNES	YAWN	SKATEBOARDS
SEA	FEELING	ROARING
BILLOWING	EELS	HOCKEY STICKS
BAKING	MONKEYS	CLICKING
SAILS	GEESE	STARS
TOES	GRAVE	MOONSCAPE
CHEER	MY AUNT	SUNSPOTS
RAKING	ANCIENT	WEEPING
BREATH	JEALOUS	UNPLAYED
MAGIC	CELLAR	PIANO
RAINBOW	UNCLE	EARTH'S RIM
APPLE CORE	FERRY	WILLOW
PEACH SEEDS	BOUGH	BLOOD
FIGHT	RUB-A-DUB	SHOUT
TRICKLE	CANOE	OPEN WIDE

DUAL OF DOVES
APPLE PIE
BARLEY OATS
SCULPTOR
CRINGE
CRAFTY
DRAFTY
BEHIND THE ALTAR
GO SLOWLY
SHARPER
SWALLOW
CRUTCH
YELPED
CURIOUS FACTS
KICK
FLOCK OF
BELIEVE ME
SWEETNESS
JAGGED
MOONLIGHT
CROOKED
PUMPKIN
SQUASH
VIOLET
SNAKES
DINOSAURS
SNAPDRAGONS
FORTUNE
BOOM
BLAST
SKIN
BLOSSOM
FEATHERS
WAITING ROOM
ANGRY
FIERCE
ROARING
BREATHING CREATURE
STEMS
GREENEST
VIOLIN
PINE CONE
RIVER BED
OPEN
DODGES
PERCHING
QUIRK
OUCH
WOUND
CUT
FOUNTAIN
SPRAY
SILVER
WALKING
RUBBING
FRECKLES

A WHOOSH
ZONK
TWISTED
SAFFRON
THE BACK PORCH
I AM
BALLOONS
STRINGS
FATHER ROCK
WATER SPIDERS
MUSTACHE
PANTING
THE SCENT OF
NOBODY ELSE
TOADSTOOL
YOU CAN SLIP
SPEECHLESS
MUSCLES
BONE CHILLING
GRAB
GROANING
TOOTH
ANXIOUS
CEREAL
NOT TOO LONG AGO
ONCE
WICKED
WRIGGLED
MUSHROOM
HAVING DINNER
FLOPPING
LEAPING
FLYING
YOU CAN'T BLAME
UNDER THE
THE EMPTY BANK
A SINGLE COW
CLOSED DOWN
AFTER THE PARTY
MY MOTHER SAID
MY FATHER SAID
WHEN CAN I
GOSPEL SONGS
CHURCH DOORS
SOUL FOOD
BURRITOS
SPICY CURRIES
POTATO PIES
FRENCH FRIES
BBQ RIBS
CALLALOO
GRANDPA
GRANDMA
ABUELITA
ABUELA
MY HOMELAND

MY ROOTS
REMEMBER WHEN
LISTEN
JOIN ME
FOLLOW ME
OPEN THE DOOR TO
LOOK!
WE PLAY WITH
LULLABY
TEDDY BEAR
DOLLS
TENT
CLUBHOUSE
TREEHOUSE
TREETOP
SHADY SPOT
SUBWAY STATION
BUS STOP
DRIBBLING
BITE DOWN
IN GREEN HATS
TASTE IT
OF MY MIND
HER CLAWS
HER TEETH IN
THE BIRDS WILL KNOW
SHUDDER
JUMP UP
TWO FEET HIGH
THREE HABITS
ON TOP OF THE STOVE
MY BLUE RAINCOAT
ORANGE AND BLACK
THE RIBBON BESIDE
THE
IN MUSIC
SLIDING DOWN THE
INSIDE EGGSHELLS
BUTTERFLY WINGS
WHEN I AM OLD
SILVER SNAKES
FIRE IN MY
BESIDE MY
ALL THE WAY AROUND
PARTY
MAD AT MY
UPSTAIR
FIRE ESCAPE
YES YES YES
THE WAVES
A SLIPPERY
LEAF
INSIDE THE FACTORY
BROKE HIS
OH NO
OH YES

WHERE
WHY
PLEASE TELL ME
I HATE
MADE AS A
YOU ARE
MISTY FOREST
SHADOWY
YAPPING
FOGGY
STICKY
PRICKLY
CRACKLING
BIG WAVES
BAREFEET
HAIR FLOWING
HAWKS
SLITHER
WIND
FLYING FISH
SAIL BIRDS
FLUFF
SEEDS
SCARES
DROPPED
OVER
FLAPPING
SLAPPING
MAPS
MOPS
TALKS
SCAMPERS
PLAYS
SLIMY
FLIES
PILLOWS
BROTHER
DUSK
WORDS
EMPTY
GRACE
ROOTS
SOIL
EATING
TASTING
TIDES
CURLING
KISSING
SHARKS
MUSSELS
FOLDED
SWEEP UP
SCATTER
INVISIBLE
PLEASURE
CRICKET

EACH OTHER
MOONSONG
SUNSONG
RAINSONG
EVENING SONG
SAD SONG
IN FLASHING
WAVES
IN SILVER
WILLOW WAND
HAZY MORNING
RUSHING
SANDMAN
MUD
BILLOWS
SISTER
TWILIGHT
SCRABBLE
HALF MELTED
SNOWFLAKES
DRIFT
DRY WIND
SPIDERS
THORNS
SEED PODS
HANGING
BANGING
PLASTIC BAG
RED HOT
PINEAPPLES
LAUGHING
GROWING
TOUCHING
WRINKLES
ISLAND
STAGGER
LIFELINE
FLAGPOLE
UNIVERSE
PLANET
SPACE
STARLIGHT
BESIDE
TRAILING
STOP AND GO
IN SUMMER
TROUBLED
NIGHTMARES
SQUEAKS
SCREAMS
SCRAPES
WHINES
FACES
HILLSIDE
SIPPING

DAWN
DEER
STONES
CLACKING
PEBBLES
SWAMP SOUNDS
NARROW
GREENING
BAYBERRY
CRANBERRY
TOMORROW
YESTERDAY
NOT YET
AWAKE
MIRROR
SNAKESKIN
RESCUE
SWELTER
SPINACH LEAVES
GIRAFFE SPOTS
WAR
FIRE
SUNSET
TRIPPING
IN THE LAP
HUSH
PENGUINS
DREAMS
LIES
WISHES
POEMS
TWINKLE
SWALLOWS
LUCKY
WILTS
EYES
ROADSIDE
SIDEWAYS
IN THE DAWN LIGHT
SEA MONSTERS
PURPLE TIGERS
HUMMINGBIRDS
THAT DAY THERE
WERE
PINE TREES
BEHIND BROKEN
WINDOWS
BLOOD IN THE
SINGS ALONE
THE LIGHT IN THE
SIX ARMS WAVING
HOUSE
SAY
YOUR CHEEKS
PAPA

MAMA SAID
BEST FRIEND
A LARGE
IN THE DARK
THUNDER IN MY
JUMP INTO
SMOOTH STONE
LEPT
TRIED TO
WANDERED AWAY
FROZEN
IT'S EASY
TAKE IT
FROM ME
UNDER THE BRIDGE
MAYBE A FISH
TOMORROW IS
I CAN'T KNOW
WHEN IT ARRIVES

Then give the children a few minutes to make up a poem. Read them out loud and see all the variations you can have, given the same words. The children will quickly get the idea and be anxious to try their own poems.

> *my mother says*
> *why*
> *I say*
> *why not*
> *we swelter and dip*
> *until maybe a fish*
> *shudders*
> *says shshshshsh*
> *says when*
> *says under the blue*
> *fence*
> *you are both*
> *Mr. Pigs.*

> *Elizabeth McKim*

EXAMPLES OF WORD BOWL POEMS BY CHILDREN

These poems have elements of the real magic of poetry, of language working on a metaphorical as well as a literal level. Sometimes the twists and turns of the unconscious mind give to language a second level of meaning, deeply true and most personal. When a phrase particularly strikes you or the child, talk individually with her about it, emphasizing the specialness of her statement, sharing the discovery of self-expression.

> *I wonder if*
> *roses begin*
> *as a blossom beneath*
> *honey, fur, and two voices*
> *in the next town*

> *Susan B., 4th*

An excellent way to get the children started is to pick, at random, a list of ten or so words from the bowl and write them on the board. For example:

> *says*
> *when can*
> *I   my mother   shudder*
> *why not   swelter and dip*
> *etc.*
> *swelter and dip*
> *maybe a fish   you are*
> *too   shhhh   blue fence posts*
> *Mr. Pig*

> *How   ham*
> *I   on*
> *wish   our*
> *he   own*
> *was   little*
> *my   love*
> *uncle   hill*
> *eating*

> *Karen*

44

My Fingers

brush up my fingers
with blue snakes
of the hill

my fingers are so cuckoo
so what said my mother stemming a water-bug
but my fingers are going cuckoo
go to the moon said mother.

A little girl
with blue strings
born on the edge of
the hill.
She was crying
summertime
flies.

Lyn Bigelow

Hazy morning
Angry hawk on the back porch
talks

Nancy Manning

three apples release their
mother's love

Lyn Bigelow

Dinosaurs stutter
in the forest

Ronnie Fronduto

A pale face
A pale face
like a salty
green apple.

Laughing wolves
Laughing wolves
on an island
waiting for
starlight sails.

Peter Lee, 5th

Girl

One
day
when
Superman
came
at
dusk
On
the
back
porch
nobody
else
but
I
saw
him
my
hair
was
blowing
The
wind
closed
the
door
the
wind
sounded
of
pirates
rushing
in
panic
of
Superman

Janet Kohn, 4th

Stop sister
trust me
Listen to this evening
song
Look at that round
planet
trailing swallows.

Connie Vieira, 5th

44

Why

nobody else scares
false maps
off my face
as well as you

nobody else whistles
spinach leaves
rustles seed-pods
as well as you

nobody else sings
the songs I know
so simply

Elizabeth McKim

Have on hand large pieces of drawing paper, markers, colored pencils, and crayons. Bring the bowl around to each child, and have her pick about fifteen to twenty words, spreading them out on her drawing paper. Urge her to experiment, to try all kinds of combinations. It is not necessary to rhyme in these poems or even worry about making complete sentences or complete thoughts. We are more interested in 'surprising images' or words that have a special sound pattern. There is no required length. The rules are very flexible. If the child doesn't like all the words, she can turn some back and replace them. She doesn't have to use all of them. She can repeat any she wants to. She can trade with a friend. If she needs a few more, she can get them. She should add words herself here and there, if needed, but avoid putting her words together in sentences which would defeat the goal of making a poem.

When the children get their words the way they want them, ask them to write them out on the drawing paper the way they wish them to look, using the markers and crayons. They can draw if they wish, and weave their words through a picture. The combinations they will get from the word-bowl will delight them.

When the children are reading their word-bowl poems out loud, I might comment on a line that strikes me. I might ask them to try a poem using that line or using one of their own lines as a first line.

As work with the Wordbowl progressed, I began to see how important it was for students to find their own words, in fact to be "word/gatherers." So I send them outside to hunt for words: verbs and nouns: the essentials of strong poems. I ask them to look at everything around them, to listen, to smell, to touch and hold and to write down persons, places and things: these clumps of language, these building blocks called nouns. Write them on a piece of paper giving each word space to breathe and be. Bring along another paper for the verbs: the motion, commotion, activity, slight murmur or trembling. Observe closely. Be specific. When you have filled two pages, one for the verbs and one for the nouns, come inside and tear out the separate words and start your poem, making choices, exercising your "artist-mind," playing with the form and line, deciding what and if you need to add: adjectives, adverbs, qualifiers, pronouns. This is the time of serious play. After your poems are done, you have a good beginning for your own wordbowl which you can keep adding to as you gather more words through experience and reading.

During the study of particular Native American tribal cultures, Susan Harmon, a second grade teacher in Brookline, asks her students to create a word bowl of words and phrases associated with the culture they are currently studying. This focus allows children to integrate content from social studies units and to use appropriate images and beliefs in their poetic expressions about a particular culture. This activity can be adapted to the study of almost any culture: Eskimo, Japanese, Russian, Nigerian, and so forth.

Yesterday
uncles of the old ways
in the desert —
Earth's rim,
watching peaceful
painted clouds
drip
moisture for corn.

Boris Abemelik, 2nd

FIREDRILL POEMS

One of my favorite beginnings is this word association exercise named for the speed at which it has to be written. It works best the first time when the children have no inkling about what is going to happen. Sometimes I tell the children I am going to give them one word and they should write down everything it makes them think of no matter how crazy it may sound. I give them a word. HURRICANE. They have one minute only to free associate. When the time is up, and only then, do I tell them to make a poem using these words as a basis and adding others as they like. The idea is not to make structured sentences or thoughts from the words so much as a collage of associations about that word. It is almost like creating a word bowl yourself in one minute. The range of results is also amazing.

Hurricane

The Heavy, Rainy, Disaster
Dorothy from Kansas died in it.
Wind heat, fast speed,
pain, injuries, sickness.
Screaming women find dead cows
and chickens' bones.

David Brillhart

Sometimes I pass out a slip of paper to each student, giving each a different word. I try to use evocative words, words that convey a vivid image or have strong connotations and associations. CROW, KNIFE, WILLOW, STARSHIP, ICICLE, PRISM, LION, KITE, TEAR, WOUND, JAIL, SNAKE, STONE, FOREST, RIVER.

Crow

The ocean screams and howls
and birds and eagles fly high
and the birds
sometimes look like swords.

Ann Rutkauskas, 5th

Crow

Crows drift over fields
of golden sunburned wheat
black wings hide in trees
while farmers scream with rage,
in flight crows steal over
golden grass.

Aaron MacArthur, 5th

Wind

When the wind blows
the confusion is soundless,
the sound of confusion is
the breeze blowing through the
tall tall grass.

Doug Cormier, 5th

Making Connections

Making connections is at the heart of poetry. If I say that the sky is blue, you probably won't even hear me. If I say that the sky is as blue as a robin's egg, you might look up, but I won't count on it. How about an African violet? You give me a funny look. You think of the velvety purple of the petals. If I say the sky is melted marbles, you think of the marbles you rolled around in your hands as a child. But why melted? And then you see the merging of all those colors: blood red, cobalt blue, sea-green, streaked or flecked with white. Suddenly you hold *my* sky in the palm of *your* hand.

One of the things we try to do in poetry is to tell someone else about who we are and how we see the world. We want the people who read or hear our poems to see us and our experience as clearly as possible. One technique for achieving this is to make comparisons. Comparing one thing with another, making relationships, is a natural part of speech and of life. "When I'm lonely I feel like a little dried leaf in someone's pocket." "When I'm sleepy, I am laundry which blows in the wind." "When I'm angry, I am mean as a hungry alligator." The important thing is to make comparisons which will allow someone else to understand what you feel and experience.

Comparisons help us to use all our senses. If I say a potato chip tastes salty, you might say "big deal." But if I say it tastes as salty as tears, and as crunchy as crickets, you know a bit more.

Saying that the wind through the iron gate *sounds* like a flute tells you more than saying that the winds sound scary. A stone *feels* like cool silk. Lemons *taste* like a field of crab grass. Water-melon *tastes* as cool as a waterfall.

Be specific. The relationships are always there. We just have to find them. This is why poetry is useful, a basic tool for communication; it allows us to understand more deeply who we are and what we mean.

The idea is to make comparisons that will surprise the reader, make him think about what the poet is trying to say, and reflect the feelings of the poet toward the subject of the poem.

Examples:

I am a milkweed seed.
I look like snow with an ant on me
drifting down from the sky on a winter day.
                                    2nd grader

The Bark

It's like a dancer dancing heavily
with its dress going every which way
or a mad river crashing against rocks.
It feels like a pine cone all flattened out
and on the other side it looks like a cliff
or a mountain with all different textures
and also like a cannon cracked in the middle.
The color looks like a dark storm cloud
about to break with rain.
When I shake it, it sounds like a creaking
door, being opened.
                                    Leigh Bigger, 5th

48

My barn in Vermont is as dark as a spider
and I can hear birds singing so sweetly
I can feel the cobwebs hanging from my ear
I can see the bees tangling in the web
and I still dream about my barn in Vermont.
                                    Mara McCue, 3rd

March 1st

Coming out of the house on a fresh March
                morning,
I saw February still meandering around
like laundry caught in a Bendix. Stray shreds
of cloud, like pillow slips, were rent from
her large endlessness. Outdated,
her decrepit body garlanded itself dis-
gracefully with powder. She luxuriated in old age.
Even her graying sheets were still there,
tattered, heaped carelessly on the street,
bearing the indentation of someone's huge body
and furred with a fine fringe of soot.
She had been plump, she had been heavy, sitting
on top of us since January. Winter, you
old clothes hamper, what mildew
still molders inside you before March
dribbles a bit, dries up, and is done for?
                                    Kathleen Spivack

Tears

Tears,
    Tiny
    salty
    seas
        of
        s
            a
                d
                    n
                        e
                        s
                            s
                    and lost hope
rolling gently off the tip of
noses,
        down
                cheeks
dripping off chins
tumbling
            miniature
                    seas of despair
                                    Karen Wilder, 6th

Celebrating

The ice breaking on the lake
I walk once
each way around

the blue white crust
shrinking like outgrown skin
cracking a black river
through the center
like a split lip

walk once
        and down in hollows
        giggles
        girls on bikes in packs
        lovers in sweaters
        boys dangling like new leaves
        from trees

each way
        a magic dance
        of dogs and old men
        with sticks clicking
        clatter of skates
        jingling of bicycle bells
        music of the lake breaking

around
        the edges
        the sun works
        along with small boys
        dropping pebbles

walk once each way around

already worrying words
                                    Judith Steinbergh

Looking at these samples, we can pick out the comparisons, and see how the poet has made us see things more sharply.

The poet perceives the world in terms of comparisons. She sees the light turn trees into humans, weeds into stars. She casts a spell and turns the light on the lake into a jar of fireflies. You will never see the lake or the jar of fireflies in quite the same way again.

BODY

There are various ways to get children to feel comfortable sharing comparisons. One is by talking together in a circle, using metaphors and similes as the structure through which we talk.

We start with the body, something we all own. We all open our hands. Then we close them. We make a simple movement with them, a movement we can all do. Out of the movement comes a sound or a breath. We examine the lines on our palms. The knuckles, the joints, the fingernails. How similar and different we all are. I begin, free associating, letting whatever image pops into my head be spoken and shared, even if it's not totally exact or appropriate. "*My* hands are two feathers blowing in the warm air." "*My* hands are two squeezing sponges." "*My* hands are sea anemones." "*My* hands are baseballs." "*My* hands are gold fish." "*My* hands are two soft sounds." Students are watching. They are interested. As they listen to me making these comparisons, I can see their own minds are beginning to travel. One volunteers, "My hands are like two octopuses." "My hands are like steamshovels." "My hands are pieces of bark fallen from a tree." Soon they all want to share. One idea generates another.

Quickly we move to another part of the body. How about the head. "My head is a spaceship filled with computers." "My head is an empty gymnasium." "My head is the inside of a crater." "My head is a mountain lake." I ask them to close their eyes and to feel their heads, the shape, the weight. We all move our heads.

My neck is a big paper towel tube.

My legs are a peace sign. My toes are teeth that don't bite. My toes are ten flash cubes. My toes are pine cones. Gems in a mine.

We go on to different parts of the body. Our feet. Our belly buttons. Our arms. Our hearts. Blood. Bones. Veins. When I sense that we have talked enough, I urge them to go off and write about their own bodies, making comparisons. They can either choose one part, or do a whole catalogue of the different parts of the body. They can draw the shape of the body or body part and place the words around or inside of it.

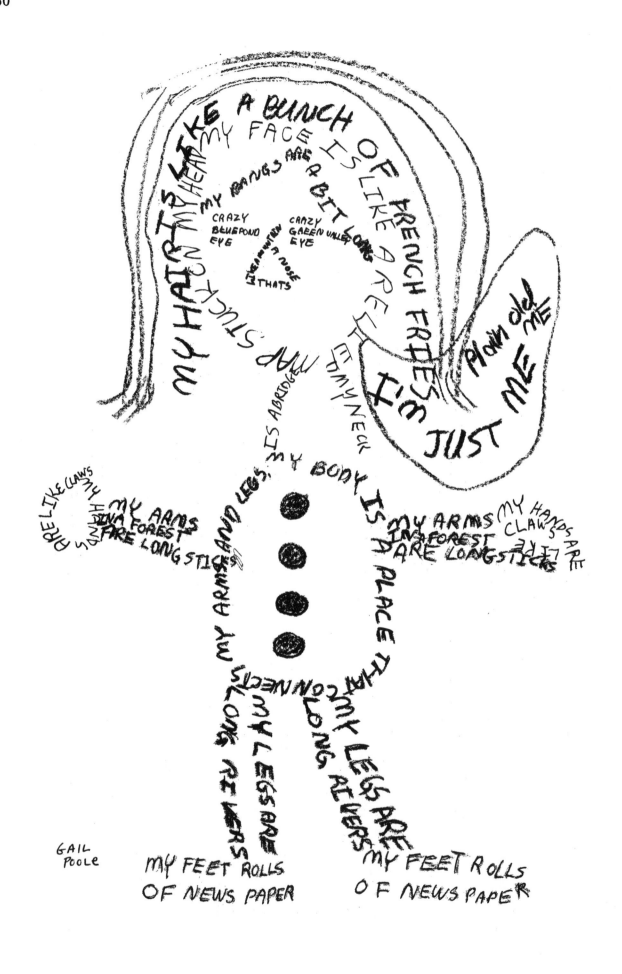

GAIL
POOLE

My legs look like a tree.
My toes look like roots.
Don't worry.
I'll grow.

Boy, 4th

I think my heart is
a pumping machine with
straws taking cherry
juice that goes to
a room where it lives.
One room has five things
sticking to it.

I think my brain
is a busy machine.
It sent letters
to every room in my body.

Boy, 3rd

Who Am I?

My tunnels are carrying my fuel. If I have no fuel,
I can not run. When one of my factories stops
running, the other one starts. I have two lookout
posts. They tell me if someone is trying to shut
me down. The main computer is on the top floor
and if I don't have a computer, I can't run.

Joe D., 4th

Fingernails are like hard rocks.
They are shaped like potato chips.
Some fingernails are as long as sticks.
My fingernails are connected to my hand.
My hand is like a lily pad with a frog sitting
on it.
I have little snow balls on my hand.
My hand is connected to my arm.
Like a tunnel with cars going through it.
My arm is connected to my shoulders.
My shoulders are like big mountains.
My shoulders are connected to my neck.
My neck is like a tube of tooth paste.
My neck is connected to my head.
My head is like a round baseball.

Kathy Bell, 4th

When a couple of children have finished, I ask one to trace another on a huge sheet of paper. Then we hang up the traced body and put the poems up on the appropriate parts, poems about hands around the hands, poems about brains around the head and so forth.

This is a collaborative poem made by the fourth grade at the Countryside School in Newton, Mass.

Our Bodies

My eyes are like shining crystal balls.
My eyes are like golden rocks shining
in the moonlight.
My eyes are two goldfish,
are two sweet apples.
My eyes are like white diamonds with brown
emeralds in the middle.
My eyes are the centers of sunflowers.

My ears are like two loud speakers.
My ears are endless caves.
My ears are like cups drinking up a flow of words.
My ears are like seashells from the sea.
My ears are a tape recorder that won't
stop recording.

My nose is like a mountain in the country.
My nose is like a silver slide going down.

My hair is black thread running away.
My hair is a golden river falling down the falls.

My mouth is like a red leaf on a tree.
My lips are the color of God's heart.
My mouth is a long, long, long, long
tunnel.
My mouth is like a word bowl.
My mouth is like the Cave of Never.

My teeth are a cage in my mouth.
My teeth are the albinos of my body.
My stomach is a moaning machine
that moans whenever I get hungry.
My toes are flesh-colored teeth
that don't bite.

My heart is a beating drum,
My head is a ball of thoughts,
My heart is like the end of a road.
My brain is the king of my body.
My head is the shadow of the moon,
My hands are like doves, soft and gentle.
My neck is the twister of all my bones.

52

Hands

My hands are shapes: doors, wonders!

My hands are as soft as a moth.

When I am shy I turn purple
And I like to touch soft things.

When I hook my thumbs together
They remind me of a colorful butterfly
That flies through the air.

> *Third grade Collaborative Poem, Lynnfield, MA*

FEELINGS

You can try the same sort of structure with feelings. "When I'm angry I feel like a huge storm brewing up toads and snakes, hurling rocks into strange places." "When I'm angry I feel my feet are so heavy they will kick a hole through the earth." "When I'm embarrassed I feel like un-cooked spaghetti is caught inside me, even in my mouth." "When I am lonely I feel like I am a closet with no clothes in it." "When I am scared I stay inside my shell like the sea-urchin with all my prickles out." "When I am happy I feel like a locomotive going down the track." "I feel like a clear lake on a bright October day." "I feel like a cherry on top of a banana split." How do *you* feel?

Children know what you are talking about. We begin to share. Joy, confusion, dullness, boredom, amusement, questioning. How do you feel? What is it like for you? I bring poems by other poets, both children and adults, chosen to express feelings.

When I am happy
I feel like a new mother
and new winter snow.

When I am sad
I feel like a dead flower
and a winter with no snow.
I feel like a raging fire
and those are
my feelings.

> *Mary Hogan, 6th*

When I'm happy
I feel like
a stream
with children playing in me.

When I'm mad
I feel like a
tea kettle burning.

> *Margaret, 6th*

When I'm happy
I feel like a sailboat
with my sail up and
the wind is blowing up against
me. I feel proud.

> *Catherine Powers*

When I am sad I feel like a
car when it runs out of gas.

Join Me in a Better World

Join Me...
in a place of laughter
where the music is joyful
and where the sound
   of happy children rule.

Join Me...
in a place of fun
where the sun feels so good
where people live in peace.

Join Me...
in a place where people see new
things everyday,
where people are not racist
It's for me.

Jamaa Strickland, 4th

FEELINGS
By Jenny McKim
Age 9

DIRTY
I feel like a fish
Out of water
all oily and scaly

HURT
I feel
like a bee
Just stung me

HAPPY

when my best friend
Couldn't come over
I felt
like
a burning pile
of tears

when I'm happy
I feel like Bambi
When he goes out
in the Open field

When I'm mad
I feel like
a crocodile
who just
missed a fish

Glad
When I'm glad
I feel like
a pink bunny
with white ears
who just found
a patch of carrots

Excited
When I'm excited
I feel
like a Mexican
jumping bean

When I'm afraid
I feel like a piece
of popcorn
who just popped
out of the pan

When I'm sad
I feel like
I just slipped
on a banana
peel and
fell into
my birthday
cake

When I'm proud
I make a big
smile
And do whatever I'm
sposed
to do

When I'm sorry
I feel like a pig
who just got a tummy ache
because he ate too much bread

When I'm Yelling
I feel like a Dragon
Burning Out
his yell

After I've been
Yelled at / I feel
like a chipmunk who
drowned in
his own tears

TIRED
When I'm tired
I have a fight
with my eyes
because I don't want
to go to bed, but
my eyes just
get heavier

When	*town*	*a pocket*	*my*	*like*	*my*	*of*
I	*I*	*my pocket*	*heart*	*a*	*face*	*fire*
am	*have*	*is*	*is*	*bed*	*is*	
happy	*heart*	*my*	*soft*		*a ball*	
my	*it*	*heart*	*it*			
face	*is*		*is*			
feels	*like*		*soft*			
like						
a						

Boy, 4th

Feelings

When I'm mad
I feel like a cannon ball
Sailing through the air
And hitting the ground

When I'm in a bad mood
I feel like a goldfish
Playing the theme
of Rocky
on the guitar

When I'm mad
I feel like a cat
That took a bath
and got all wet

When I'm sad
I feel like
An ejected salami sandwich
That got all moldy
And ditched in the trash
barrel

When I'm silly
I feel like a drunk clam
Doing the chow-chow

When I'm embarrassed
I feel like a king with a diaper rash

When I'm happy
I feel like a pig
Who got Italian dressing
On his bread

Robert Diotte, 4th

When I am sad I feel like
leaves all crumpled up

When I am lonely I feel
like the only apple in the bag

When I'm mad I burn up
like a hot stove on fire

When I'm scared
I feel like in the movies. I
hope it doesn't happen in real
life.

Boy, 4th

WRITING ABOUT YOUR EMOTIONS

Being able to write about your feelings in a way others can share is as important as the ability to reason. Speaking about an emotion in the abstract, "I feel sad," does not convey the uniqueness of your experience or the quality of your sadness.

I reinforce the idea that specificity is vital to the poetic statement. I like to introduce ways to write about feelings by focusing on the common feeling of loneliness, which is an emotion we all, adults and children, have had to face at one time or another. I begin a discussion of times children may have felt lonely: perhaps they were lost in a department store, their mother went to the hospital to have another baby, a parent went away on business or left home, they moved to a new town or a new school, a best friend moved away, no one would play with them on a playground or they were having a bad time at a party, an animal they loved ran away or died. From this discussion, most children can remember one time they felt lonely.

I ask them to imagine they are directing a play where a child is feeling lonely. Without having the child say "I am lonely," how can you indicate by visual and sound effects that the child is feeling lonely? Where is the child? By the ocean? In the woods? In a city alley? What time of day is it? What sounds might you hear? Trees creaking? Fog horns? Owl hooting? Sirens and gun shots? Wind through the trees? Would there be shadows? Bright lights? Fog drifting in? Would the child be alone or with others or with an animal? Your emotions affect how your perceive the world. You might see things differently in the same location, depending on whether you were feeling lonely or happy.

I was lonely now
because I am sad. I am
lonely tomorrow because my
dog died Oct. 20, 1980. I am lonely
and not lonely. Like one
animal in a cage or one
flower on a hill. It is lonely
to be alone. I am lonely
Sunday Monday Tuesday
I am not Wednesday Thursday
Friday and am just in the middle
Saturday. But today
I am happy.

Chris Kleeman, 2nd

When I am sad
I sit on the porch
and think to myself
and say how it is going to be
when I grow up
is it going to be wild people on the earth
or just me

Susan B., 4th

When you feel lonely, what else are you like? One egg in a nest, the last berry on a bush, a kite caught in a tree? When you begin to write, try to focus on one incident and record what you saw, felt, heard, and smelled. How do you feel in your body and in your mind?

I am lonely as dead leaves rustling
by a cold, light, far away breeze,
on a cold misty day.

As lonely as Boston's swan boats
waiting for the arrival of Spring.

As lonely as when you wake up
at midnight after a nightmare, and

you can't find anybody.

lonely lonely lonely lonely lonely

James H., 4th

Once children understand how images convey their emotions more powerfully, they will be able to apply this tool to poems dealing with every emotion.

Complete Sadness and Loneliness Poem

I'm alone in my house and
I can't find noise, chirp or
cheep. Sadness comes to my
mind. I call my dog and
no answer comes to me
and I realize my mother
has taken him. I try to bring
happiness to my mind but
it fails and instead it
sends tears to my eyes.
I feel as lonely as if there
is no one on the Earth
and then I think it is
true. I look outside and
the air is lonely and only
three cars go by.

Robbie Myers, 4th

Happy

Joyful smile, I leap in the air
I will do anything my mom says,
I will do my chores I will practice my flute
I will paint the sky
I will climb the highest tree
I have a feeling inside
that just lifts me up!

Lara, 3rd

Nutty

Jump for joy.
Dance for peace.
Laugh for fun.
Just jump and run.
Do big leaps in the air.
Just mess up your mother's hair.
Hug your cat.
And put on a fancy hat.
Put on your mother's old coat.
Put on your brother's favorite tie.
I'll tell you once, I'll tell you twice,
You look so nice,
You're nutty, why oh why.

Johanna, 3rd

As I sit up in my tree
I feel lonely
As I look out I see the lake
I see a boat go by
It is quiet
I look to the other side of me
It looks peaceful
I hear a squirrel
Run up a tree
He is quiet
I feel better now
So I leave

David Fisher, 6th

OUR ENVIRONMENT

Now we move on to describing our surroundings. Description in poetry is never completely objective. It always reflects the poet's feelings or attitudes toward his subject. As poets, we want to communicate to someone else how we have experienced an object or event. To do this, we must be as specific as possible. If I tell you I've seen a weed, what do you picture? It might look like this (I hold up a cattail) or this (I hold up the dried remains of Queen Anne's lace) or something entirely different. How do you know what I've seen? But if I compare the weed to something specific, you will begin to understand. I saw a weed that looked like a chocolate popsicle. I saw a weed like a star. The comparison makes a kind of puzzle. It sets your imagination in motion to guess why I used that particular one.

What about a shell? You haven't the foggiest notion as to what my shell looks like until I tell you that my shell is like a cupped hand, or flat as the moon, or curled inside itself like a secret stairway.

I read the children my poem about a cattail, which uses all the senses and as many comparisons as possible.

The Cattail

It looks like a chocolate popsicle before it melts
It's as tall as a giraffe and stiff as an icicle
It feels rough like a cat's tongue
and smells like fall flying in the window.

It sounds like a cat, quiet, purring
and rustles when the wind blows.

When a cattail goes to seed
it is like a puff of smoke
or a buffalo
or your grandfather's beard
It feels like cotton candy at the circus
It floats apart like clouds
and flutters down like raindrops
It looks like an explosion.

It lives where its feet
are always wet
and its brown velvet head
looks over
the green geese filled swamp.

Judith Steinbergh

We all bring in our treasures to share. There are weeds, reeds, shells, branches, stones, vines, seed pods, that we have collected. There are gourds, bayberry, bark, sponges, lobster claws, bean pods, sea urchins, and star fish. There are fossils and marble and agate and sea glass. We also bring other objects: a clay pot, bells, swords, strings of beads, and a woven belt. Everything has an interesting shape, texture, smell, sound or taste. Dried fish from Chinatown nearly knock you over with their smell. Cinnamon, tarragon, clove, onions. Hand-like roots of ginger.

I ask the children to pick one object and sit with it for a time. Look at it carefully, its colors, its form. What else does it look like? Close your eyes. Touch it all over and think what other things it feels like. Shake it. Smell it. Then write about the object using comparisons wherever you are able. Tell me what it looks like, sounds like, feels like, tastes and smells like. How does it make you feel? I want to experience this object as close to the way you do as possible. You might even write from the point of view of the object.

Fossil

See I am

> *new moon in a night sky*
> *fingers grasping rock*
> *life after life*
> *until it melts*
> *makes a mark*
> *veins in a flattened face*
> *wrinkled voice*

Touch I am

> *rippled as sea*
> *foothills before peaks*
> *cold as forest over forest*
> *the back of the moon*

Smell I am

> *buried in pine*
> *needles pine cone*
> *in thick resin*
> *under the tang*
> *of sassafrass and mint*

Taste I am

> *tongue of the earth beetle*
> *hidden until flicked*
> *forked into sun*

Listen I am

> *silent*
> *as constellations*

Find me

> *I will blossom*
> *many spores*
> *many secrets*
>
> *Judith Steinbergh*

EXAMPLES BY STUDENTS

The pot looks like a pear with a mouth
The pot's color looks sometimes like the sky
with wind around it.
The pot smells like clay with vanilla mixed.
It feels like a rough rock with a hole.
It is hollow like a cave.
I can fit a genie in it.

> *Ann Rutkauskas, 5th*

The Shell

A curled, burnt-in-places marshmallow.
Inside, it's the finest, whitest cream,
of the most white goat in the world.
It smells like lightly-burnt charcoal
with a dash of incense.
As bumpy and ridged as uneven cement.
Bare trees and paths leading to
an enchanted white mountain,

with a cliff curled about
like a spiral staircase.
An ice cave surrounded by dirt and snow
Part of it like an eye with eyelashes
pricked up.
Pricked up in spaces like
unmixed (well, not very well) cake mix,
pricked up by a spoon.
The color of a coconut-macaroon cookie.

> *Vicki Hood, 5th*

A Huge Pine Cone

The tips look like dips
of an ice cream cone.
They curve upwards
like a witch's fingernail,
and are as sharp as needles.
They go into the middle and disappear
like roads going away into the distance.
It is long and round like an egg.
There are drops and crystals of sap
like a raindrop with the sun shining

through it
The points are light tan like a peach
The insides are dark maroon like an
  oak leaf.

  Sarah P., 5th

I am a seed pod,
I smell like an abandoned house.
I am as dark as the night.
I look like a doll's hat.
I sound like a baby's rattle.
I grow in a lake.
I stand on a lily pad.
Frogs jump on me.
I taste lousy.

  Stephanie Dimock, 5th

Waves

They curl around like a high round "C"
Making sounds like nothing else can,
Speaking their own language
The beat in the heart of the earth.

They are the home of living things,
The summer fun for everyone.
They are wet, salty, cooling and
  white capped,
Colored in blues and greens.

They are the waves!
Yet, they are mine.

  Kathy Cogan, 5th

A Glass Bracelet

It's a rounded square
An owl's eye
Rusty red
An old, forgotten
key
No one has used
In the rain
Shiny like our
bannister
A clown's ring
To juggle
Flat on the edges
It smells

Like a scrubbed table
Fingerprints
A crystal ball
The world.

  Valerie Berger, 5th

Horse Shoe Crab Shell

It's hind entrance has two prickles
sticking out like reptiles keeping
out visitors.
The shell itself looks like a lung,
the holes like a rapid fire of
bullets or as if it was sewn
together but then the thread was
taken out. There are sharp pricks
sticking out on the side, like
daggers and holes in between. It's
color is like ancient pottery that's
been underground for years.
It looks like a bat without head
or tail or a chest protector.

  Ricky Miller, 5th

SUBJECTIVE vs. OBJECTIVE WRITING

Another interesting exercise for children in fourth grade and up is to choose an object which attracts and interests them, look up the dictionary definition for it, and then write a poem about it, choosing details and comparisons which reflect their feelings toward it. They can leave the two descriptions separate, or weave them together. For instance, the encyclopedia has this to say about milkweed:

Milkweed

The family is of little economic importance; however, the floss of some species has been used as a substitute for kapok. Local use is made of the plant for food, medicine, dye, and fish poison. The common milkweed, often a troublesome weed . . . . .

This is the definition of milkweed or what is called the "denotation." Elizabeth's poem about the same subject examines the associations she has with milk- weed, what we call the "connotations."

Elizabeth McKim's Poem
**(from Woman With Milkweed Meets Man
From Deep Inside Whale)**

*We lie together in a huge space
  and feed on milkweed,
found high in meadows after summer
  small fluff-seeds in a bark canoe,
packed and ready to take off.
  Milkweed! Catapulting out the spout-
hole like rice at a wedding, quilting the sea
  with field dreaming, tossed high and higher;
spiralling up into the mean wind
  and gnaw of gulls, like lazy curlicues
of smoke. We turn the sea, we turn
  it into more than what it is,
and what it is is more than we can know.*

Witnessing (For Patty)

*Beneath leaves of a plant that's named for milk,
that bleeds milk, we search for chrysalides—
things that I've never seen, but whose name I like.
And I think, as I look, of all the things*

*you've taught me to name—larkspur, loose-
strife, sea lavender, plants called hens
and chickens, butter and eggs, your eyes
bright with such knowledge, and solid as nouns.*

*Just so, you tell me now of creatures
who choose the underbelly of these leaves to make
wombs of, studded with gold, from which emerge
Monarchs that range the length of the Atlantic*

*in hordes—one more fact I must have missed
by skipping the fourth grade. And when, today,
we find no trace of anything resembling this
miracle you mention, and I'm about to say*

*you made it up, you bend down, break a pod,
and blow unlikely butterflies in the sky's face—
not black and orange like Monarchs, but cloud-
thought white, or like the way I mark my place*

*when I read your eyes, which, witnessing, claim:
This is the world. Try to learn its name.*
                              Gary Miranda

Forsythia

*any shrub of the oleaceous
genus Forsythia, native in
China and Southeastern
Europe, species of which
are much cultivated for their
showy yellow flowers,
appearing in early spring
before the leaves.*

This reference book definition of "forsythia" uses very different language than this portion of a poem by Ruth Whitman.

(from) Stealing Forsythia

*I came back with the sun smeared
  on my hands.
A yellow guilt
Pulled from my neighbor's bush,
Ten yellow branches
Moist with guilt and joy
Caged in a green vase on the piano
  top.*

                              Ruth Whitman

In ways such as this, I point out the importance of both objective and subjective writing in learning about and assimilating the subject matter. Sometimes I have children choose an object, write a detailed description of it, measure it, weigh it, etc., then draw it as carefully as possible and finally write a poem or myth about it. One kind of learning without the other seems to me to be only partial learning.

62

Object: a chain of whelk shell egg cases

Objective description:

It feels brittle and rigidy
with a rough texture.
It's about one foot long.
It has a rattling noise.
It has little chips on it and
they look like banana chips.
Its color is like a tannish-white.
The little chips are like a bubble
and in it are little shells.

Andrea Walczewski, 5th

Poem **(subjective description)**

My object
is a long brittle thing.
It reminds me of a snake
It also has a shaky noise
almost like a baby's toy.
My object is very dry.
Whenever you hold it,
it feels like it is
going to break,
  "crack!"

An Exercise in Listening

EXERCISES IN LISTENING

"Your ears can't hear what my ears hear!" says a four year old in Jacqueline Jackson's book, *Turn Not Pale Beloved Snail*. Two people "can be in the same spot, ears exposed to the same noises, yet they will be getting different messages."

Here are several exercises that help children sharpen their listening. These isolate the sense of hearing so children can concentrate only on what they hear.

HALL SPYING

I send the children into the halls in teams of three or four, stationing them at different places (outside the office, in the basement near the boiler, outside the kitchen, outside the library or kindergarten, near the front door). With paper and pencils, they are to sit quietly and record every sound they hear. This includes fragments of conversations, phones ringing, typewriters, footsteps, pipes gurgling, comparisons to describe what these sounds are like. For example, if they hear loud pounding footsteps, they might say, "footsteps like a herd of elephants". If the footsteps are soft, they might say, "I hear footsteps like cotton balls falling." Sometimes it takes a few minutes for them to hear anything at all. Children should not worry about organizing these sounds, just record them as quickly as possible.

The following is an example of what might be recorded:

The boy's footsteps sound like thunder. The furnace sounds
like a fan. People talking upstairs.
Mister Joiner whistling. People running upstairs.
Doors squeaking.

> *Amy Dodge, in 2nd. grade.*

OUTDOOR LISTENING

Spend some time sitting quietly out of doors. Record only what you *hear* and what it sounds like: birds, wind, trees creaking, traffic, dogs barking. You can do this with words on paper or notate the sounds with your own made-up symbol system on music paper.

Have children try this exercise at home, at the supermarket, in the bus going home. You can imagine you are hearing the sounds in the world for the first time. Or you might imagine you are an animal, a cat, for example. What sounds would you be most conscious of, and how would you react to them? What sounds would you want to store in your mind if you only had three more days left to hear?

What are all the different sounds of rain? Rain like bullets against my window, rain like fingers on my face, rain like waterfalls over rocks, etc.

How could you describe different kinds of silence? The silence in a class when no one knows the answer, the silence in your room before you fall asleep, the silence in the woods before a storm.

Jacqueline Jackson says, "We're all selective

listeners, but most of us select too little and don't
vary our selection from time to time, don't turn
the knob."

Los Pajaritos

Los pajaritos cantan
pero no se les entiende nada.
Todos los dias me pregunto
que estarán diciendo.
Ellos hacen nidos
pero yo no los miro.
Todas las noches ellos me cantan
pero yo no les entiendo.
Pajarito lindo, nos vemos mañana.

Elizabeth Salgado, Spanish Bi-lingual 4th

Hear the Sound

hear the sound?
yes I do, the spring
sound.

hear that sound?
yes a pond is
melting and going on a trip.

hear that sound?
yes a tree has
many new babies

they are saying
we have a new
bright shirt

hear the sound?
the grass is
coming out!

the birds are
flying up the sky
All the animals
are waking!

Grace Yang, 5th ESL

Rain

Listen to the sound of the rain
drop drop listen to the rhythm of the rain
rain is something that stops and ends
It is something that you can open
your heart to and just listen
It reminds me of a song.
It reminds me of a bird singing.
I name rain the symbol of singing.
It gives a beat.
It gives me a feeling that I can't put in my mouth
It gives me a feeling in my heart
Rain makes me sad but
a different kind of sadness.
It gives me a feeling not just inside
but out.
It makes me just want to sit down
and fall into a deep deep sleep.
    Rain.

Suzanne McKay, 5th

Suzanne McKay discussing her poem with Judy.

Special Places

We talk about special places, places we return to in reality and in our imaginations. We read poems by younger and older poets about places.

The Cellar

I love my cellar with its dusty smell
Its misty smell like smoke rings
From clouds blowing past,
With its shelves of jams and goodies
With its boxes . . . barrels . . .
Woodpiles here and there.
There is a passageway
To an unknown room
Where bins hold carrots and things
There are glass doors that bang
And cobweb windows
I love the quietness of my cellar
Thinking in the dark.
My cellar has apples in its breath,
Potatoes even
That smell of earth.

Hilda Conkling

Knowing and loving a place demands a special sense. Bring to mind all the associations with that place: the sounds, smells, colors, the shape, the space, and texture of the place. Who goes there and why? Is it private or do you share it with others? Perhaps it is a place which has been important to you from very early childhood. Perhaps it is a main street of your home town, or a place in your school, or a room, or a corner of a room, or a secret place you go to be alone, or your bedroom, or cellar or kitchen. Maybe it is a barn, or a tree, or a fort in the woods, or a meadow, or an island, or a pond. Maybe it is a place you make for yourself in your mind when you want to get away. Choose a place you have an intimate connection with, for whatever reason, and see how much of it you can share in words. Bring all your senses into play. Scraps of conversation, dreams, daydreams. The light and shadow surrounding your place are all important.

Examples

As I go to Portland, Maine,
I see apples blooming in my spot,
Whistling wind, weeping rivers,
and blue skies.
Can I call it paradise?
I think I should because
wind blows, grass is green,
and in the woods, misty green
but in the winter white as can be,
fawns running, bunnies free.
Can I call this place paradise?

Patty Berry, 6th

My secret place is in the woods
where it has a purplish darkness.
I can smell the trees growing.
I can feel the bats snoring.
I can see the dust collect
where I can feel myself think.

Colin Steele, 4th

The Beach

The hot sun.
The wind blows
the sand in the ocean
and you're eyes.
Sand castels lay
in the sand. You
make streams
with the ocean
and the sand.
You swim in the
ocean and float
on you're back. And
the whaves go high

5/30/81 by
David your son

1st. grade

David Steinbergh, 1st

68

The Farm

The farm
What a peaceful place.
The tree house
crunching and creaking
as you walk.

The cat stalking
in the grass.
Flies buzzing through
the humid musty air.

The wind
is a treasure
every small breeze
treasured in a box.

The loft is the hot particles
absorbing into your skin
until you despise it,
you can't stay in this
wretched place.

The meadow with its
little prickly stubby
stalks punctuating
the bottom of your bare feet.

Sonya Gropman, 6th

My sister and I sleep in our tumbled rooms,
and our parents sleep together,
fingers intertwined.

The second stairway's narrow.
It darkens when I close the door
behind me. And I climb up to the attic,
to the bustles and pantaloons
hidden in trunks, the diaries and love-letters,
the photographs, the rings,
the envelopes full of hair.

Here's the old silverware
Great Aunt Irene and Uncle Eric used.
Her fork is curved
from her life-long habit
of scraping the plate.
His knife is broader,
the better for buttering bread.

Here are the bookcases of discarded books:
Tarzan, Zane Grey, a textbook Shakespeare,
piles of National Geographics, Look and Life:
enough to last me a while.

I sit on the dusty floor
and open a book.
Dream music fills the air
like the scent of dried herbs.

Marilyn Waniek

Sometimes I begin by having everybody relax and shut their eyes. I ask some of these questions:
You might imagine that you are waking up in your special place. What do you *hear* first? Is it birds, trucks, a bell buoy? What sounds tell us where you are waking? Now what do you smell? Fog? The woods? Bacon cooking? What kind of light is there? Coming through a tent? A bedroom window? A fort in the woods? Now what do you feel on your skin? Finally, open your eyes. What do you see?

Herbs in the Attic

A cat by the fireside, purring.
But I don't stop there; I go
through the living room and up the stairs.
My little brother stirs in his crib.

My Favorite Place

I awake to the sound of my dad's truck
Like a mad tyrant in a pit.
I hear the crows caw and the sparrows whistle.
As I sit in the garage half awake, I smell a faint
    smell
of bacon and dampness. I feel mist all around me
    cold,
like an ice cube melting on your back. I taste dust
from an old drop cloth I use for a blanket. I see a
    squirrel
in the window cracking a nut, though hard as a rock
    rock, he opens
it and thinks what a fine meal. Yes a garage is a
    strange place
to be, but it is the favorite place to me.

Brian Archibald, 6th

After writing about a place you know well, try writing about an imaginary place or a place you have never been, maybe a place you have always wished to see. I hand out scraps from a National Geographic map with lots of foreign places on it. I also have a list of strange names in the U.S. The children can choose one and create a special place, just from the name.

Devil's Hole

In my home town Devil's Hole
60 people stand alone
There is a place
where you can bowl
in my home town Devil's Hole
where 60 people stand alone.
I want to buy an ice cream cone
where 60 people stand alone.
I would like now to see a phone
in my home town Devil's Hole
All the people pitching coal
where 60 people stand alone
in my home town Devil's Hole
I do not like my home town, No
I want to leave it, yes, right now
I hate my home town Devil's Hole
I hate it when we pitch the coal
I hate my home town Devil's Hole
where 60 people stand alone.

Mark Barret, 6th

My Thought Sanctuary

As I lie
between a mixed up sentence
the coats do a dance,
for anything I order
they will answer.
That wardrobe is funny
but does me well
as servants in my
Thought Sanctuary.
The pictures
belong on the wall,
they are my thoughts
they belong in my Thought Sanctuary.
Oh no, the eyes
of a curious criminal are coming

to break me open.
Alas, I am safe
in my Thought Sanctuary.

Lyn Bigelow, 6th

Poets sometimes use a phrase to invite the reader to journey into the poem or to accompany the poet to a special place. In Robert Frost's poem "The Pasture," he ends each stanza with "You come too." Ask your students what phrases they can think of to invite the reader to come along to their special place. Some examples include: Come with me, Follow me, Join me, Open the door to a place where, You are welcome here, Look, Listen, and so forth.

Trinidad

Come with me to where the air is sweet,
Full of tropical scents of mangoes,
    papayas and curried coconuts,
Come with me to where the pebbles
    and sand are beneath your feet,
Where the trees gently sway in the summer breeze,
Where the trees are covered with minty green leaves,
Where the sun shines brightly in the morning light,
Where the crystal clear oceans twinkle
    in the evening light,
Like scattered crystals in the night,
Come with me to where the air is sweet.

Catava Franklin, 4th

My Tree House

Come with me to my tree house
where you can look beyond the city where the
dangling stars are at night where you can look beyond
the sea, Come with me to my tree house where you
can smell the freshness of the air
where you can
see how peaceful
the earth is
where you can
hear the birds
singing and
the stars dancing,

Come with me to my tree house
where you can feel the earth
where you can touch nature.

Christine Chang, 4th

Persona

OBJECTS AS PERSONA

In many tribal societies, a person has a "bush soul" as well as his own. This "bush soul" takes the form of a wild animal, tree, rock or some other existence in nature with which the human identifies. A person may be convinced he is both a man and a lion. As Carl Jung has pointed out, this ability to relate closely to nonhuman life has been civilized out of us. Often children and adults can be freer and more expressive if they can return to a less rational logic and imagine themselves to be something or someone else.

Forsythia Hum

I'm a family of 19 bursting suns
　falling
　　　falling
till we reach the ground,
bees come humming a tune
of pollen sadness. It is day
of night when I wake,
I am in the heaven of flowers,
it's a lovely sight
of friends singing,
heaven of forsythia hum.

Lindsey Freedman, 2nd

The use of a persona allows us to say what we might not ordinarily reveal. Masks provide us with ways of internalizing metaphor, extending imagination and becoming more truly ourselves. There is an endless number of such persona; some of these include objects (natural and man-made), vegetables and animals (real and imaginary), and the lives of other people.

In working with persona, you can rely simply on what is around you: a crumpled piece of

by Kirk Martin

paper, a stone from the playground, the crack on the wall, a lost sneaker, one glove.

There are potential poems everywhere. In high summer, they lie hidden in kelp among rockweed at the high water mark. They are in moon shells, conches, thin golden jingle shells, crisp black skate cases, the khaki armor of the primitive horse crab, translucent chains of egg cases, silk-gray driftwood. In the sandy soil, I find thickets of bay and blueberry, their strong scents released by crushing them between my fingers. There are poems here.

Poems wait in pebbles, in black-and-white marbled rock worn smooth as a cat, rocks grainy as oatmeal, slate worn thin into arrowheads, mica from Vermont, cracker-thin rock from the Arctic Circle, and salty rocks from the Dead Sea.

Bittersweet

I was once growing on a vine.
Now I'm dry,
Dead almost.
I have been near a tree,
Down a path,
Up some steps,
In a room by a chair,
And onto a table.
Now I'm in a vase.
My face is orange, my ears, yellow.
I have many arms.
I hope I never die.
As I am on the table, out the window I gaze
Down the path and
Through the woods to the willow maze,
And just beyond, I see the vine,
Alone, where I once played.
                                    Tricia Newell, 6th

We might feel ourselves connected to a lightbulb, a clay pot, knife and spoon, a leather hat, a ball of yarn, a pincushion, a broken music box, a Raggedy Ann doll with a painted-on heart, one ice skate, one bicycle key, a carved box from China, a hammer, a clock, a Christmas tree ornament, a string of beads, an old map of England, a candle, a windchime. These things that surround us are the poet's booty.

Windchime

I am a chinese windchime
I hang over a chinese garden
The wind tells me when I can speak
But I tell me what I can say
No one else knows what I can say
Not even my brothers and sisters
I say my own thing in my own way
That's me singing sweet nothings.
                                    Edward Knopping, 6th

A Broken Flute

Before- I used to have a sound
My own sound
Slipping and mixing with myself
All day - just clay
Gentle hands gave me a special noise
To please friends of those hands
I was taken from my home the lands
Now all I do is clatter when I roll
Clunk when I fall
Just a broken flute.
                                    Nick Rasher, Age 16

In class, I introduce each object to the children. We spin tales around things, imagining their births, life process and endings. The children's curiosity is touched; they are anxious to see what is coming next; they are deciding which object they want to be. This ritual, the turning of "good junk" into treasure, and the start of a relationship between the children and the objects, is as important as writing poems.

I ask the children to take their time with the objects, to stay with them for a while. This watchfulness, I say, is part of being a poet. I ask them to choose something they can identify with, something that shares some of their own characteristics.

When they are ready to write, I give them guidelines such as these: Be the thing you are writing about. How do you smell and feel? Imagine where you have lived and all the changes you have been through. Do you move among many others or sit very still alone? What does it feel like to be a lightbulb, being turned on and off? What does your shape remind you of, and what is your relationship with candles and the sun? Are you one of a kind? Do you have your own sounds, language, special songs?

Clay Pot

I feel smooth on the outside
and call like a mourning dove
when the wind blows upon me . . .
                    Mary Beard, 6th

I read them examples by my students and a few poems by adults. These children write convincingly about life from behind their masks:

Candle

I am a dark blue candle
smooth and tall
When I am lighted I am happy
and have a warm feeling inside.
But when I get blown out,
I get a cool misty feeling.
                    Edward Knopping, 6th

Flower

I like the sun
I like water
I open up me
to the water
Bees like me
I have honey inside me
I am pretty
I am purple and orange
People pick me
People eat me
I like the flowers
around me
People like me.

                    by Flowers
                    and by Shauna Steinbergh, 2nd

(from) The Life of a Feather Duster

. . . I also have dreams that in heaven there will be
dust and even in death I will wipe away the dust.
Will there never be enough dust. I sigh. I will
just be swept away in the sadness of dust.
                    Margaret Danielle, 5th

Driftwood

I drift through the water
very slowly like a smooth piece
of felt, floating in the air.
Sand and water go through me
while dead fish land upon me.
I am like an old man at the end
of his years. I crack and I chip
when every wave hits.

Tim Nance, 6th

Anger

I am anger, hot mean, stormy, anger.
So many people express me
at times. Even at times when
there is no need for me
But I hate goodness
happiness, gladness.
My concern is only
for evil, deep hot evil,
So many things calm
you down when you are angry
I fight to keep people
angry
But my fight is a losing
battle
Anger! Anger!
Let your anger show.

                    Ellen Ramirez, 6th

Dried Seaweed

I am so very complicated and
            prickly,
Disorganized, yet organized in
            ways.
My arms reaching out for some-
            thing hidden
swaying with the slightest
            breeze or movement
I have hardened with the years
            and now
will not sway as easily.
I have seen yet have no eyes.
I have heard yet have no ears.
I have learned.

                    Marianne Vaccaro, 6th

Carrot Scraper

Lying there listlessly
Surrounded by half-clean
Can openers and measuring spoons
and jabbering twisties,
The drawer bangs open.
Slender, well-manicured hands
pick me out of the disarray.
The smell of carrots
sustains me; it

lets me know that
once again, I will scrape off
all pretense
revealing only the sweet inside.
Pretense is balled up
and thrown into the
kitchen waste basket.
The carrot scraper
had done it again.

                    Valerie Berger, 6th

It is also possible to give children words for objects which can't be brought in to class or held. My words include: tear, face, faucet, window, wound, sailboat, cliff, lighthouse, bathtub, water, fire, air and earth; mountain, valley, cloud and storm; door, willow, wind, rock, house, icicle, prism, kite, firefly, quilt, iceberg, moon, cave, tide.

Water

First a drip
a baby
Then a creek
a toddler
Then a stream
an older child
Then a river
a teenager
Then a bay
a young adult
Then finally the ocean
an old person.

                    Deirdre Brown, 5th

Tear

The eylid opens like a secret
            opening.
A bit of dust comes in.
I am comfortable until I slowly
            drip like water
forming stalactites and stalag-
            mites,
I clean the dust off.
When someone is sad, I call my
            friends
and we gush out like a miniature
            waterfall.

                    Ady Kendler, 5th

I Am a Small Box

I am the small box,
in me is everything.
Including everything there isn't.
There are aliens in me and
there are unknown things
in me like fookachins
and splatter buzzards.
There are even wizards
and sorcerers' powers and magic,
thoughts and imagination.
I hold the future, present and past.
I have myself in myself,
NOTHING is not in me!
Fright and fear,
bravery and braveness,
knowledge and stupidity.
I also hold what's outside of me.
I can change the impossible
And that's just about all.

Matthew Kovner, 2nd

I Am a Porsche (a rap).

I am a Porsche,
I am so fresh,
my design is red,
and I am the best,
I ride around
all day and night,
I don't go put - put,
I ride just right,
and my master is a girl,
who looks so fine,
she has a shape of a body
that will blow your mind,
I have black and white seats,
a red and silver trunk,
a guy crashed into us
'cause he was drunk,
My master put on me
a pink license plate,
even though the color pink
is the color I hate.
We ride around the state
that is our fate,
when we get home ,
we get home very late.

Danny Cintro, 6th

VEGETABLES AS PERSONA

Fruits and vegetables provide lush and immediate sensations, shapes, colors and textures. Food is close to the emotional life of children, and again, it provides an abundant set of masks through which the children can talk about their feelings.

(from) In the Root Cellar

To be a green tomato
wrapped in the Sunday book section
is to know nothing. Meanwhile
the wet worm eats his way outward.

The apples are easy abutters
a basket of pull toys and smiles
Still, they infect one another
like children exchanging the measles.

The beets wait wearing their birthmarks
They will be wheeled into the amphitheatre
Even before the scrub up, the scalpel,
they bleed a little.

I am perfect, breathes the onion.
I am God's first circle
the tulip that slept in His navel.
Bite me and be born.

Maxine Kumin

The expense of bringing in a variety of fruits and vegetables for a whole classroom may be reduced by having each child bring in one fruit or vegetable, trying to make sure there is not too much duplication. You, as teacher, may want to bring in a few of the more exotic ones: artichoke, pomegranate, kiwi fruit.

As we take them out of bags, one by one, we talk about them: The apple has a star inside and poisonous seeds. The banana bruises easily. Someone looks up. The eggplant is smooth and royal, inside, spongy pulp. Look at the layers of the onion. As soon as you discover one, there's another. The garlic. Either you hate it or you love it. Someone else looks up. What happens to the potato when it gets old? Eyes everywhere. The beet is hairy and bleeds some. Feel it, bite into it, hold it. Daydream around it. "And now," I say suspensefully, "The cauliflower . . ." "It's a brain!" someone yells.

The scarlet coat of radishes, the peppery whiteness inside. The flesh of a grape held up to the light, the compartments of the pepper. Artichoke. Art I Choke. The heart of it. I save the pomegranate for last. I cut it in half, and as the juice spills out, everyone shouts, "It's bleeding." The children handle the food, deciding which one they want to be.

I am an onion. I am so mean I make
everyone cry. My skin
is like being in the sun for one million
years. Inside me is like a cave with
so many peeling doors that go on forever.
But one day they come to a shape that stops.
                                              Girl, 5th

We make a pact to become vegetables for the morning. No one refuses. Some of the poems are beautiful and really talk about feelings. Others are whimsical. Some are halting, but there are real attempts to take on a strange new being. However, the real success is not a finished vegetable poem, but a new awareness of something in our everyday lives.

Lemon

They try to tell me I'm not what I think.
They dye me and feed me full of their things.
Conform me.

> *I am myself.*
> *I am fresh and sunny.*
> *Me.*

They take me and reap me. Stamp me.

> *Sun kissed.*

They use my juice. Squeeze my life out of me.
They take my scent to clean dishes and make
hands softer.
They use my seeds to grow more.
They throw away my skin, my shell. Nothing left.

> *I want to peel my skin off and show you*
> *the sun!*

Well damn you. Yes you
I want you to see me.
You don't know me.
Don't say I'm fake.
I'm not unreal.
I am me!
                                    Amy Rosen, 7th

Onion

My eye like an onion
layers at a time peeling off
as each layer comes off
more reality comes true
yet I feel I know myself
more and more
as each layer comes off
but I also realize
that as each layer comes off
more and more I grow
and far far away.
My layers allow me to know myself
Also they protect my secrets
In a way
I am proud
of my distinctive smell of
        awareness
                                Heather Garret, 6th

Radish

Once quite pale
As Someone sampled me
Now quite red . . .
Tinted by embarrassment.

                    Catherine Miller, 7th

Brussel Sprouts

I'm like a tightened fist. Holding
back all my anger. Trying to stay closed
and trying not to open and explode
with anger. I can't hold my leaves
closed any longer. I'm exploding. My
leaves are opening. I feel like
a rocketship that just took off for
Mars. My outside leaves are green
but my innerself is yellow with fur.
Now that I have been rid of my
anger, I can now return to
the field and start all over again.

                    Boy, 6th

Corn on the Cob

hairy hairy hairy
on the outside
lumpy lumpy lumpy
on the inside
smear on butter
when it's done
chew on the right side
chew on the left side
chew it chew it
till it's gone!

                    Peter and Bob, 6th

Cabbage

my mind is as complicated as
           a cabbage
each new layer a new thought
           struggling to make its
           way out;
no one can quite understand
for I am the one who actually
knows each layer.

                    Karen Hoffman, 6th

Onion

clear
colorless
circle
a ring
of smell
my
skin
tanned
and
lined
my
hair
straight
and
light
my
inner
body
filled
with
thoughts
and then
my inner
core
my heat
my heart
my tear

　　　　Tirzah Nardone, 7th

An orange.
　　Sweet, tender.
　　Above all it glows prettily in the morning sun.
　　At the end all that is left is the skin
　　and the seeds.
　　Its thoughts, its inside feelings all
　　given to someone else.
　　Its loving kindness all given away
　　A mother.

An acorn squash
　　Tough and everlasting on the outside
　　Nice and juicy on the inside
　　It also goes like the orange.
　　Its thoughts and feelings given away.
　　A father.

　　　　Kyle Pedersen, 6th

Artichoke

I build up my protection,
　　　　layer after layer
I put sharp points where their
　　　　fingers will pluck my pieces off.
Really what I'm hiding most
　　　　　　　　Is my heart.
　　　　So tender it is.
Still they eat me.
　　　　It must be hard
　　　　I must admit.
Every layer they peel right off.
　　　　Ha! Ha!
　　　　the outsides too hard!
The teeth scoop out my tender inside
　　　　anyway.
　　　　So much work for so little food.
Ohhh my h
　　　　e
　　　　　a
　　　　　　r
　　　　　　　t

　　　　so soft and silky
The prickles didn't stop them.

　　　　Nothing can
　　　　Nothing will.

　　　　　　Diane Hurley, 6th

ANIMALS AS PERSONA

　　Animals and made-up creatures are an effective persona because of our natural affinity to them. Most children have loved at least one animal, and they can share the excitement of its birth, what they imagine to be its life, and, in some cases, its death.

my antenna feel
like sticks my coat is
a rat. I am an awkward bug
but that's the way I am, I
don't know how to fly
but my friends all come
and tease me but when the rat comes
my eyes feel like dropping to the ground
Here I am catching my breath for the next
　　　　trip around.

　　　　　　Girl, 7th

Runes

Like green sea turtles I swim oceans, stroke
       through open
water, my carapace borne up by water, my soft
       flippers
pushing down water. My long head held forward I
       float
like an island taking in air. My kind always near by
rising and diving as I rise and dive, floating we
       sleep
the sea birds screaming as we rock.

I have fought waves landed on beaches and
       heaving my
terrible burden of shell have oared through sand
       to where
I buried what roiled in me to come out. I have
       left eggs
on many beaches, clashed and coupled with my
       kind,

rocking down churned waves where the fish glint
       in the
moonlight and the shore burns and the long boats
       come.
I swim free on far paths of ocean and come home
       to
island shallows.

Now I am alone. My flippers draw in, my head
       comes
back into my neck, my slow eyes veil. I am into
       my
shell. I drift and then am thrown, grating on sand.
What within me has been taut and tense lets go.
       My
leather legs and arms slide out, my head rolls from
its neck. In the blue sky the birds gather. My shell
no longer contains me. I choke in the hot air and
       the sea
has sent me out.

Margery Cavanagh

My life is long, sad, and dark.
I am a buffalo with the great body
Big enough to knock down a tree
But I wasn't strong enough to get free
We where plenty when man came
But now we are few.
We've been shot, slaughtered, skined, and clean
But will never die like once before.

Demedrick Williams age: 11

I talk about what animals can do, habits that seem both peculiar and endearing. We talk about the long migration of the whale, the bat's sonar hearing, the longevity of the elephant. We read some animal poems together, Randall Jarrell's bat poem, a few of the animal poems of D.H. Lawrence and Ted Hughes. Most poets have written at least one animal poem, and it's fun to look for these.

Sometimes we try some theatre games. Each child chooses an animal to become and the others guess who he is. One hatches from an egg; one changes into a butterfly; one stalks her prey.

Or I might bring in animal pictures. We talk about them and each child chooses one. I ask them to be that animal and tell as much as possible about its life and feelings. I remind the children that the poem-animal can perform, if they wish, unusual feats, things that the real animal might not do.

Hi I am a bat
I'm not like other bats
I'm crosseyed I don't hang
upside down by my feet
I sleep upside down on my ears
and I hiccup like this hik hik hik hik
when I fly
instead of flying on my wings I fly on my ears
I don't eat meat I eat hot coke
and I eat cotton candy with syrup
when I'm happy I fly around and around in a
circle
and smile I say etetetetetetetetet skweeeeeek I
am red and black I am funny
                    Boy, 4th

Are you big and frightening? Where do you live? Are you a hunter? Who are your enemies? Describe yourself. (I remind the children that they can determine what their animal looks like. If they want a zebra-striped canary, fine.) Are you going extinct? Do you travel in a pack? Do you have a family? What do you hate to do most? What do you feel like? (We close our eyes and imagine the slimy skin of a frog, the dry dusty feel of a snake, the scales of a fish.) What do you sound like? We try a dialogue between two sounds. This could be a whole poetry experience, along with listening to records of animal sounds, whales and wolves, birdsongs, zoo sounds, etc.

The children imagine what the animals are saying: lullabies, lovesongs, fights.

The main idea is to get the children to feel an identification with their animals, whether a made-up creature with a strange name and its own special language, or a real animal brought into focus by the needs of the writer.

The Rick Rhino

The rick rhino
lives in a big cave
and all he does all
day is sleep and
at night it
eats popcorn
and watches
the football game
on t.v.

rick rhino
has a friend
Dicky Dicky Dino

Their language has
three words

Moo
*   Nah*
*   Jup*
                    Boy, 4th

A Lone Wolf

A lone wolf with no companion
The sun shining reflecting off the snow
makes his fur seem glossy, thick, soft and warm.
And his eyes show wisdom and wildness,
but kindness, loneliness and sadness.
Isn't he something like me?
He is strong, cunning, skillful
but merciful and gentle.
He faces the elements
that make him mighty
For he has no companion, no mate,
and no leader. He lives
but barely. It is his wisdom,
his kindness, his loneliness, his sadness,
his mercy and his gentleness that makes me
feel pity and love for him. I say again,
isn't he something like me?
                    Chris King, 6th

The Boy versus the Rabbit

I, the hunted,
am scared half to death.
I never did anything to hurt anybody.
Yet here I am, being hunted by a boy.
I shouldn't be scared,
boys can't shoot.
I'm not scared . . .
Oh yes I am.
Help, someone help me.
If he would be nice
I would be nice.
Hey, he stopped.
He put down his gun.
I should run while I can.
But I can't.
Something makes me stay.
I feel close to this boy.
He slowly advances towards me.
I run towards him.
Stop! Stop! I tell myself.
No.
This boy is nice.
I jump in his arms.
He holds me tight.

Cilla Smith, 6th

The Eagle

Me the eagle with my keen eyesight
*   and strong wings.*
I devour the sky. I build my nest
in the highest tree to watch the
land below. Suddenly on the land
below I see a rabbit in the corner
of my eye.

I open my wings and swoop down
like a rocket.
I pick off my catch like a lion.
Then I rocket off to eat in peace.
When I see another eagle,
I swoop down to fight like a bear.
Then I go home to fix my wounds.

Scott Patch, 6th

OTHER PERSONA

The possibilities are limitless. Here is a brief summary of several other approaches that have worked well.

OCCUPATIONS: The class lists unusual occupations: deep sea diver, sky diver, pianist, poet, garbage collector, lion tamer, beggar, butcher, baker, candlestickmaker. We include their parents' jobs: carpenter, lawyer, teacher. I read sections of Robert Hayden's "The Diver" or the following poems.

Trapeze Artist

When I climb the rope
all my sequins sparkle
like water in bright sun.

The spot light follows
like a cat rubbing against me
with its yellow fur.

When I grasp the swing
all the air is mine
I arc up through the darkness

the spotlight flies with me,
it feels safe as a net.
When I am high in the rafters

I let go
rolling through the air now
my whole body

spinning like a wheel
my heart
spinning at its center

and as I uncurl
my hands meet the strong hands
of my partner

they are always
at the right spot
in a circle of light

all around us people
are cheering while we swing
gently gently from the bar

two plumed birds
two iridescent dragonflies
at rest in the sky

Judith Steinbergh

84

I'd Slide Out of My Life

sun on the door
spilling on the side-
walk to town hop
a quiet trolley
to the greyhound

terminal sleep all the way
to Iowa find a small
town with one main street
one all night diner
get a job

feeding truckers slapping
down sunny-side-ups buttering
englishes pocketing
dimes hum with the juke
till three make it

home alone
sun in a while
coming up hungry red and mean

I would lean into life
like a pilot or a dancer

I would change my name
Sundays I would bowl

Elizabeth McKim

I ask them to think about the way the people in each job interact with the world, the dangers they face, whether they create something from nothing, whether they are bored in their job. Which jobs are lonely? Which ones exciting? I ask them to choose an occupation with which they identify closely.

Pro Food Taster

Going into restaurants
all over the world
Just tasting tasting
tasting tasting
Chocolate bars, pies,
cakes, cookies, pop corn,
pizza, spaghetti, ice cream.
I like those foods best
but there's still
lots of others.

Goodbye I have to
catch an ice cream plane
to Washington, D.C.
for a taste test.

Mark Lender, 5th

Sailor

At night I hear the engine's snores
and silence
and in the distance
I see lights that flow.
But sometimes I get lonely
and I hear nothing.
The wind starts to blow
and still I hear nothing.
Then the waves come over the boat
The captain yells "drop anchor".
When that's over
I wake up from my dream
I put on my clothes
and go out to the bridge . . .

Scott Del, 5th

Clown

Clown, that's me.
Where my shadow goes, I go.
With a bright spotlight,
With a strange dot
A strange spot.
With a lot of polkadots,
Strange people all around,
Strange things all around,
I practice all the day
for when I do it
It's worth a day.
That's me all around.
That's me and I'm proud.

Sam Simon, 4th

ELDERS: We talk about old people we know, our grandparents, our neighbors, people in the park. How does it feel to be old? How would we look and sound? What would we be afraid of? What would we love? How would we walk, see and hear? We talk about the advantages of being old, our dreams, our memories. We look at photos of old people, listen to tapes of them talking. Many of my students have grandparents who speak only Italian, Portuguese, or Greek. Some of them write their poems partially in a foreign tongue.

Grandmother

Each summer your sweat ran on
the spoiled potatoes.
You washed them and soaked them
days and days for a couple pounds of starch.

Sun scorched your back
Sweat swelled your face
Joints ached you awake almost
every night.

When your servant snatched grandfather
from you and demanded to be equal with you,
in your sullen acquiescence did you
become an "Enlightened Being?"

When she tried to adopt
your beloved son,
did you lose your voice forever?

When the wicked woman from the city
frightened your five-year old granddaughter
you didn't have your voice.

You watched me leaving you
for a land for you and me.
I took my heritage from you:
the voice you lost is mine, now
grandma.
                    Seykio Nam.

Bath House

When I was young in the summer we went to the
          bath house
every day in the South End
We used to walk up a big flight of stairs

and for two cents we used to get soap and a
          towel.
We took our lunch with us and spent many hours.
I jumped in the water, did a lot of stunts,
but never swam.
We took old dresses and bloomers into the water.
The pool had salt water
I had more fun there than I can ever describe on
          paper.
                    Lena Greenberg
Hebrew Rehabilitation Center for Aged.

There are many wonderful books about grandparents and family. I recommend the anthologies edited by Myra Cohn Livingston about Grandmothers, Mothers, Fathers, Sisters and Brothers, and Norma Farber's long poem: *How Does It Feel To Be Old?*

Lineage

My grandmothers were strong,
They followed plows and bent to toil.
They moved through fields sowing seed.
They touched earth and grain grew.
They were full of sturdiness and singing.
My grandmothers were strong.

My grandmothers are full of memories
Smelling of soap and onions and wet clay
With veins rolling roughly over quick hands
They have many clean words to say.
My grandmothers were strong.
Why am I not as they?

                    Margaret Walker

Old

I'm as old as the sun
I'm as old as the wind
No one ever pays any attention to me.
They look straight at me.
I never want to go on to tomorrow.
I hold onto every day
like a flower holding onto its petals.
Tomorrow's never wanted,
It's a scary feeling that something's
          wrong
Something's going to happen.
                    Shelby Hall, 5th

MIRRORS: I bring in a mirror. Each child looks closely into it. A mirror is a moon, a lake, a tear. I ask questions. How would you feel as a mirror? Changing into every person who peers into you? Do you have eyes? Can you see into people? Or is life boring just looking at the opposite wall? Which is real, the self in the mirror or the self outside?

Mirror

Every
Time
I
Look
At
You
Look
At
Me
We
Go
Home
Together

Elizabeth McKim

WHALES: It is a rainy day. We come together in the circle. I ask the children to close their eyes and together we listen to the record *SONGS OF THE HUMPBACK WHALES*. This is complex and haunting poetry coming from these immense mammals of the sea. We hear their squeaks and rumbles, their long cries, their duets, their messages echoing out from the deep. "A whale's call is like a disappearing city's cry for help." We talk some about what we know about whales: their migrations, their matings, their raising of young, their threatened existence. We try to really listen to them, to imagine what they are singing.

Whale

Are they here?
The screechiest violins that come from Mars?
With WHOOOPS and gurgles like when you
gulp down some water
Everything's quiet . . . but then!
   umumerummm
Back comes their lonely cry of agony.

As I watch the water
suddenly
urumbuckkitchikoowee
It comes, no one is there
but me,
oooh, my spine is shivering
what shall I do?

                              Diane Hurley, 5th

When we tape these poems, I play the whales singing as a background.

Lost Whale

I call out
I'm lost (lost)
No one hears me
but myself.
My voice echoes off
the coral reef (reef, reef)
I cry, shout, look about,
my heart pounds (pounds, pounds)
Panic flowing through my body, (body)
I cry, shout, I shake with fear (fear, fear)
No one can hear
I cry, I sound so small in the deep sea (sea)
My mother, (other, other), mother!
I tire, (ire, ire), the sea grows dark (ark, ark)
The shadow, the shadow of fear,
A boat a boat, help, help! (help, help!)
I'm quiet, but I'm sure they can hear my heart.
pound, pound, (pound, pound)
A shadow looms up ahead
I cry out. At last, (ast, ast)
my mother! I cry (y, y)
Her comforting fin wraps itself
around me, (ee, ee)
My heart stops pounding and I glide away
in the distance with my mother.

                              Lisa Uhren, 5th

PHOTOGRAPHS: I spread photographs out in the middle of the circle: pictures from the *Family of Man*, photos collected from *National Geographic, Sports Illustrated, Audubon Magazine,* pictures showing space shots and microscopic detail. They are pictures which make a strong impact: a child holding a baby fox in the dark forest, a volcano exploding, a shaman chanting, children playing on a crowded street. I select a wide range of subjects: people, animals and objects, action pictures of athletes. I ask the children to choose a picture which interests them and try to become the image, to enter into the other life. Again, we try to ask and answer the question, "what is it like to be you?"

The Doll

All I do is rock in my chair
I have to keep a stiff grin, even
      when I'm not happy.
I sit here, lonely, with no little
      girl to take me out.
I'm uncomfortable with my
      starched blue dress scratching my
      gentle glass skin, like an eagle
      clawing its prey.
My tight belt squeezing me, like a fierce
      snake strangling a helpless animal.

Here I am, and here I stay.

                  Lyn Bigelow, 5th

BODY PARTS: Just as you used body parts to explore comparisons, you can use them to understand the technique of persona. This is an excellent lesson to use in a unit on anatomy.

Ear

I am an ear. I live in the city.
I hear big and little truck motors.
Little and big people's feet.
I hear subways screech.
I hear bright colors. I hear
dog whistles. Balls bouncing
high and low. I hear the birds
and crickets in the park.
I am an ear.

                Charlie Slotnik, 5th

Skin

I am skin.
I am as sensitive
as a still tub of water.
I feel everything that touches me,
everything.
And just yesterday,
I felt the strangest thing.
Under me a leg was broken,
the right leg.
I felt sorry for it.
And then way up on my face
I felt it.
I shivered, I shook, I was frightened.
And all of a sudden
the brain wanted to speak to me.
I said: The thing you felt was tears, a source
to express emotions, like if a human is hurt, sad,
happy, or maybe from a glare you let out, tears,
it could be called crying, as I said it is only a
                source
to express emotions. There is no need to be
                startled.
So now I know what that strange thing I felt on
                my face is,
tears.

                Benjamin Margolis, 5th

Eye

I look out, my door opens surely and widely,
in come the thoughts, I look through them.
And feel through them. Slowly they take form.
That boy is crying.

I am an eye, an   eye that helps, an eye that sees
an eye that feels, I catch everything . . .
everything that hurts. I give frantic calls . . .
help calls . . . and I respond.

If you are hurt and feeling bad, come to me,
share my vision, see my wisdom, and catch a smile.
I am an expert. A master at feeling and seeing.
You are welcome.

I see the invisible, which is very visible.
And feel and hear your loud uneasiness.
                                        Ricky Miller, 5th

Poems of Address
Poems of Instruction

POEMS OF ADDRESS

Another technique poets have used is talking directly to another person, creature, plant, or object. "Oh storm, you hurl down the trees" or "Child, you survived like a strange cat". Sometimes these poems of address are called Odes.

Usually, when we write poems, we are addressing an 'other', whether that other be someone in our life whose understanding we hope for, an imaginary person or object, a lost person, or a part of our own selves. Writing poems to a 'you' often helps us finish the 'unfinished business' in our communication with someone else.

Yourself

Oh Field, with your grasses covering yourself,
I think you look so peaceful,
but who am I?

Oh Child, You are yourself and always will be
yourself for that is who you are
and always will be. Whatever you make
of yourself is whatever you wish.
Prove to yourself and all your friends
that you can be great, or as good as
you want to make yourself.

Oh Field, How shall I do this, to make myself
good, for it is easy for you
not having anything to worry about but
people walking on you. But I also
have people walking on me.

Oh Child, Don't let them, stop them, try
as hard as you can and make it work.
For you are yourself and always will be
yourself, for that is who you are
and always will be.

Kerry Hagan, 6th

Hips

you grew wings
I never wanted
when all the rest
of me was skinny
as a birch tree
you hummed
indecently under
grey flannel skirts
ma chose 2 sizes too big
you itched to take off
lisped vague pink lullabies
through the long adolescence
obsolescence you wanted something
Beautiful/ you wanted something
shining/ you wanted something
circular/ you wanted something
rising/ you wanted something
surprising/ you wanted
something/ singular
immeasurable/ and immensely
wise.

Elizabeth McKim

FURY POEMS

An example of a poem of address is **THE FURY OF OVERSHOES** by Anne Sexton in which she addresses the child within her who struggled with the putting on and taking off of overshoes.

The Fury of Overshoes

They sit in a row
outside the Kindergarten,
black, red, brown, all
with those brass buckles.
Remember when you couldn't
buckle your own
overshoe
or tie your own
shoe
or cut your own meat
and the tears
running down like mud
because you fell off your
tricycle?
Remember big fish
when you couldn't swim
and simply slipped under
like a stone frog?
The world wasn't
yours.
It belonged to
the big people.
Under your bed
sat the wolf
and he made a shadow
when the cars passed by
at night.
They made you give up
your night light
and your teddy
and your thumb.
Oh overshoes,
don't you remember me,
pushing you up and down
in the winter snow?
Oh thumb,
I want a drink,
it is dark,
where are the big people
taking giant steps
all day,

each day
and thinking nothing
of it?

    Anne Sexton

After reading this poem, I discuss with the students places where Anne Sexton addressed objects. What images does she recall from her childhood.

I also ask them what "fury" means in this context. What else could you feel strongly enough about to want to write a "fury" poem.

Often children are encouraged to write poems on traditionally "beautiful" subjects (e.g. flowers, friendship, etc.) whereas Fury Poems confer a structure which allows anger and conflict.

I ask children what makes them furious; perhaps it is something seemingly very small: creaking radiators, florescent lights, mosquitoes, messy desks. Something at home: broken skis, little brothers, missing sweaters, parents, homework, lost allowance. Something global: war, hunger, poverty.

I ask the students to write a poem called: The Fury of —————— (whatever they choose) and to address the subject of their poem. For example: "Oh lost sneaker, where have you gone?" or "Radiators! Why do you bang so loudly?"

POEMS BY STUDENTS:

The Fury of my Sister

Oh sister why do you
always follow me around,
why do you delight in
bugging me up the wall,
how come you think
it's fun to hide my clothes
and make me late, why
do you always invite
your bratty friends
over and scream as loud
as you can and then
at night when you get
scared come in my
room crying and then
start begging me to let
you sleep with me, oh, sister.

    Amy Kuemmerle, 5th

The Fury of Cavities

Aching, oh the pain.
Wishing the dentist would just die
poking, drilling, pins, furry
little objects in your mouth
smelly fingers in your mouth
novocaine swelling your cheek
oh, the pain of it all!

Darlene Windcomb, 6th

The Fury of Greed

Money, cash, cash, money, greed,
steal, forge, blackmail, mug,
get, give, get, give, buy, gimme,
I want, circle of gold, hostages
ahhhhhhhhhh.
Oh greed, you blend with
everything. Whatever is, you are
a part of it. Oh war, oh inflation,
oh evil, greed is a part of it.

Marc LaBlanc, 5th

The Fury of Parents

They sit on the sofa,
staring at each other,
then they start arguing
then finally after time
and time of arguing,
they get divorced,
the mother gets depressed,
and suddenly the house isn't
the same,
it doesn't seem like a home,
Just a house
with people in it,
not "family", just people.

Girl, 7th

OTHER POEMS OF ADDRESS

Many subjects of poetry lend themselves to this technique of address. Writing poems (or even letters) to people we are close to, our elders, our ancestors, objects we love, animals which attract us, part of our bodies, books we cherish, results in powerful statements of our feelings.

O Brain

If I did not
have you
I would not know how
to add or spell,
if I did not have you
I would not do anything,
I would die.
If I did not have you,
I would not know how
to get a job or how
to walk or jump or run.

Lars, 2nd

Empty Puppet

You were an empty doll.
All life had gone from your soul.

You sat on a shelf for seven years.
Not feeling or seeing or leaving,

You have never been so full of sorrow.
Not once in your life have you felt so empty.

Then you felt a twitch in your left hand.
You were free!

You had a fine time jumping and skipping
and laughing and joking up on the stage.

Suddenly the lights go low.
The show is over.

You take your place on the shelf.
And move into your world of darkness.

Jacqueline Panko, 4th

94

Magic Box

Oh Mr. Magic Box
What do you have inside,
Oh Mr. Magic Box
What do you have to hide
Are you full of acorns
Are you full of trees
Or are you full of magic
Mr. Magic Box

You are so lovely
do you try and pull
people into your love,
On the outside
you are full of
shells, sand and beauty.

Oh Mr. Magic Box
just let me peek inside
Oh Mr. Magic Box
thank you for letting me peek
ooooohhhh   it's
        CANDY!

                    Linda Scoglio, 5th

Book, you give me
rivers that wind through
      the mountains,
and big castles that touch
      the clouds,
and many animals that run freely
      in your forests,
and giants that roam the land,
and birds that sing in the trees,
and meadows wet with dew,
and the tall green grass that
      is all over your land
little holes where rabbits hide.
When fall is over you bring
      the cold winter
      and the frosty snow
which covers the trees.
The rivers freeze
      and the animals
         go to sleep.

                    Craig Seidler, 4th

Growing old together
You look at me and I see wrinkles around
      your face
You tell me stories about when you were little
And you liked horses just like me
You look at me and I see legs boney and white
You touch my hand and I feel damp cold hands
I hear you talking in a rough voice
You can't run and play with me and skin your
      knee
Your hand rough and scaley
I'm growing old and so are you
But we can't stop time and let every one else grow
      old
and we are growing old together.

                    Pam Coan, 6th

Kite

O Kite how you fly so gracefully
through the air like a bird.
How your tail swiftly flaps
in the wind like a flag.
All your colors are like a rainbow
dancing in the sky.
You're trying to get free.
You are pulling at the string,
you're free in the sky but then
you are not free.
You're doing a dance to get freedom,
the string is getting loose,
it's getting looser,
then finally, you're free.
You're flying higher and higher
and then you're lost in the clouds.

                    Lisa Boyle, 3rd

Giraffe

Giraffe, giraffe, How tall
Galloping wildly about the plains.
How do you run so fast
with towering body?

With eyes alert like stars
in the night
And in which feeding
place do you like?
Feet like hammers clambering
on the knownless place.
Where are you now?

                    Heather McCurdy, 4th

Darkness, Darkness
Ants are in their snug home
Birds are in their snug trees
Babies are born every second
Stars are shining like glowing silver
The moon is like a shiny yellow half yo-yo
The butterfly is as gentle as a lamb,
Flowers are beautiful in the night
All nature kind is very beautiful
There is no need to have a fight.

Peggy Lin

POEMS OF INSTRUCTION

Some poems use the "imperative mode" to give the reader instructions. Howard Mohr uses this technique to instruct the reader on how to behave during a tornado.

How to Tell a Tornado

Listen for noises.
If you do not live
near railroad tracks,
the freight train you hear
is not the Northern Pacific
lost in the storm:
that is a tornado
doing imitations of itself.
One of its favorite sounds
is no sound.
After the high wind, and
before the freight train,
there is a pocket of nothing:
this is when you think
everything has stopped:
do not be fooled.
Leave it all behind
except for a candle
and take to the cellar.
Afterwards
if straws are imbedded

in trees without leaves,
and your house - except
for the unbroken bathroom mirror-
has vanished
without a trace,
and you are naked
except for the right leg
of your pants,
you can safely assume
that a tornado
has gone through your life
without touching it.

Howard Mohr

I suggest that students might address their instructions to a force in nature, mixing the ordinary with the outrageous.

Sun Up

Wind, blow the sun out of the pocket of the
    clouds.
Wind, blow the clouds to the moon
Clouds, shut the moon in your pocket
Wind, blow the sun in place
Sun awake the daytime animals
Flowers, look up at the daytime light
Sun, warm the air after the night
All help daytime set.

Chris Conway, 6th

Nightfall

Wind, take the moon out of the pocket of the
    clouds
Wind, blow the clouds to the sun
Clouds, store the sun in your pocket,
Stars, awake the crickets and frogs
Wind, blow the moon in place
Flowers, bow your heads to the ground
Wind, blow coldness through the air
All help set up nightfall here.

Attack of the Squash People

And thus the people every year
in the valley of humid July
did sacrifice themselves
to the long green phallic god
and eat and eat and eat.

They're coming, they're on us,
the long striped gourds, the silky
babies, the hairy adolescents,
the lumpy vast adults
like the trunks of green elephants.
Recite fifty zucchini recipes!

Zucchini tempura; creamed soup;
sauté with olive oil and cumin,
tomatoes, onion; frittata;
casserole of lamb; baked
topped by cheese; marinated;
stuffed; stewed; driven
through the heart like a stake.

Get rid of old friends: they too
have gardens and full trunks.
Look for newcomers: befriend
them in the post office, unload
on them and run. Stop tourists

in the street. Take truckloads
to Boston. Give to your Red Cross.
Beg on the high roads: please
take my zucchini, I have a crippled
mother at home with heartburn.

Sneak out before dawn to drop
them in other people's gardens,
in baby buggies at churchdoors.
Shot, smuggling zucchini into
mailboxes, a federal offense.

With a suave reptilian glitter
you bask among your raspy
fronds sudden and huge as
alligators. You give and give
too much, like summer days
limp with heat, thunderstorms
bursting their bags on our heads,
as we salt and freeze and pickle
for the too little to come.

                                    Marge Piercy

The Ground's Green Haircut

Get out the scissors and trim around the trees
Put the clouds in bags so it doesn't rain
Get the lawn mower and cut the grass
Clean out the cuttings
Let out the clouds
spring the soap, wash the hair
Turn the sun on to dry it.

                                    Scott Patch, 6th

Yet another possible format for a poem of
instruction is this poem by Morton Marcus:

Learn to be Water

learn
to be
water

direction
is any
way
you can
travel
your shape
whatever
you
naturally
become

*let the
moon
strum
your
belly
the planets
beckon
and
tug*

*learn
to be
water*

Morton Marcus

How to be the Cap of an Acorn

*To be a top of an acorn
you must feel the sunshine
on your cap. You must feel
growth in your body. And
get the feeling of freedom and love.
You must feel good inside
and outside. You must be happy
and sad sometimes. You must
feel the wind of love and get
the feeling of freedom. But most
of all, you must love.*

Tribal cultures often used the imperative mode in their poetry chants and songs to invoke the forces of nature. These chants might have been accompanied by rhythmic drums and shakers, dancing and masks, and woven through with magic words. *Dancing Teepees*, poems collected by Virginia Driving Hawk Sneve and *In the Trail of the Wind* offer examples of traditional and contemporary tribal poems. The poem that follows incorporates some aspects of tribal poetry.

*Great wind of the North, bring forth
     your great power
Give us your powers to us so that we
     may kill, destroy all evil*

*Mighty wind of the east
Bring forth rain for our crops
     So we may live in good health*

*Magnificent wind of the south
Bring sunshine
     so the crops will ripen more each day*

*Magical wind from the West
Sail us far out in the ocean
so we can get much fish for
our families*

*We pray to you wind god
for all these things*

Ah, kien, ah ki ti eya

Chris King, 5th

Learn to be a Rock

Learn to be a rock
To sit in the dirt for days
Without moving a muscle

To stare up at the towering trees
To look like a small mountain
To be shelter for the little bugs
    that hide under you

You could be as rough as sandpaper,
As smooth as silk,
As sharp as a knife,
And as blunt as a pencil.

                        Matthew Barzun, 5th

The Unconscious

Formula

To dream,
you don't have to ask permission,
nor cry out,
nor humble yourself,
nor put on lipstick;
it's enough to close your eyes halfway
and feel distant.
Perhaps the night dreams
that it is no longer night;
the fish, that they are boats;
the boats, fish;
the water crystal.
To dream . . .
is a simple thing;
it doesn't cost a cent,
you need only to turn your back
on the hours that pass
and cover over pain,
your ears,
your eyes
and stay so,
stay . . .
until we are awakened
by a blow upon the soul.

Ana Maria Iza
(translated by Ron Connaly)

DREAMS

Dreams are important to all human beings, but especially to children. Therefore, they provide an incredible amount of rich and abundant material for children's poetry. Wishes, lies, infinite possibilities, enchantment, magic, fear, terror, anger, desire, love, sexuality; all our strongest emotions find their way into our dreams. And children want to talk about their dreams. Start by exploring together what dreams are like.

Do you dream that you are running and you never get anywhere? Do you dream that you scream for help and no sound comes out of your mouth? Do you dream of falling from high places, or melting, or flying, or becoming someone else? Have you ever had a dream about being in a place so wonderful you wanted to stay forever, and then you wake up and find it's just a dream? And you want to get back into the dream, and no matter how hard you try, you still can't? Do you ever have such a scary dream that you wake up and you are so relieved because it's just a dream? Do you ever dream that something terrible is happening to you or someone you love? Do you ever dream you are doing some harm to someone close to you, like your parents or your brothers and sisters? (We *all* dream in these ways.) Do you ever dream you are somewhere and you don't have enough clothes, you've lost your shoes? Do you ever dream of being late for something important or missing trains or buses or rides to somewhere you want to go? What are the dreams which keep coming back? Have you ever had a dream come true, or ever been in a situation where you have felt you experienced this before and you can't quite place it, and suddenly you realize it was in a dream? In dreams sometimes things that are small become very large and looming, and things that are large, become tiny

and ant-like. And in dreams we make all kinds of connections between seemingly unrelated images. Future, past, and present can all be mixed up, and people from whom we are separated by death or distance can be with us in a real and vital way.

The closer you can get to the whole stream of imagery and energy from your dreaming life, the more real your poetry will become. This is a stream that is good to walk beside, to take account of, and to listen for in some of your waking hours. I tell the children they can write about a real dream they had or they can write a poem with a dream feeling to it. It is good to encourage the children to find a way of re-entering the dream and to write as if they have a place in that landscape. Then they *do not* have to end with " . . . and then I woke up and it was just a dream."

I have brought in many pictures with a bizarre dreamlike quality. In some instances, I make a collage, two or three images which normally aren't connected, a candle, a snail, and a sneaker. It's part of the poet's work to make the connections the way a dreamer does. Sometimes I bring in reproductions of Chagall or Magritte or other painters whose imagery touches onto dreams. When children cannot remember their own dreams, I ask them to become part of one of these paintings and invent a dream.

Anything can happen in a dream: you can float through brickwalls, or become a giant radish, or melt, or have brothers and sisters turn into muskrats or hummingbirds. We talk about death in dreams, and killing, about ghosts, and the people who play the parts of ghosts. We talk about what we share in dreams, and about the difference between dreaming something and having it be so.

About Dreaming: Note to My Students

I too
    have dreamed up a storm
        toppled my father
    turned my momma into ash
changed into a one-eyed hawk
    disappeared into morning
        melted the mirror
I too arrived at school without my clothes
    and I have run
             and remained
    in the same old dirt

Elizabeth McKim

The Frog and Toad story: *"The Dream"* by Arnold Lobel, is an appropriate one to tell kindergarten, first, and second grades before talking about dreams.

Perhaps you know of a film or a piece of music that would lend itself to the session on dreams. It has been my experience that children are ready to write after a discussion about their own dreams, where everyone has shared something, including you. Remember, the more vulnerable you become in these poetry experiences, the more the children will feel this is a common exploration.

A dream may include a daydream or a wish for a different society. In "Dream Variation," Langston Hughes creates a place where darkness and blackness come gently and tenderly.

Dream Variation

To fling my arms wide
In some place of the sun,
To whirl and to dance
Till the white day is done.
Then rest at cool evening
Beneath a tall tree
While night comes on gently,
  Dark like me—
That is my dream!

To fling my arms wide
In the face of the sun,
Dance! Whirl! Whirl!
Till the quick day is done.
Rest at pale evening...
A tall, slim tree...
Night coming tenderly
  Black like me.

Langston Hughes

ぼくはいつも夜 10時にねて朝6
時におきます。その間は、ゆめを
みたりします。昼間とくらべて
みじかくかんじおきるとなんだか
1時間ほどしかたっていないよう1
感じます。

Naohisa.

Students who speak no English can participate in these exercises which classmates communicate through drawings and hand signs. These poems, which many of us cannot understand, enrich our knowledge of poetry through the music of their sounds and the striking word symbols of some of the languages.

A Cloud that Cried

Not too long ago I had a dream
Of a cloud that cried.
She cried only when she was cold.
One winter night the snow came
Down, and she had fallen to the ground,
And when I went out in the morning,
I found her sitting near a rock crying
So I took her home and took care of her
And when I died she went to heaven
With me, like a sneaky little mouse.

                 Carole, 5th

A dream is like
a palace of information.
Some are good
Some are bad
Some are scary
like you were livin
with the devil
It feels like you were
dreamin of the future
like your mind was not there
but your body was
That's how I feel.

                 Philip, 5th
                 Su Reece,
                 Hartwell, Lincoln

A person without a dream
sleeps like a rock.
But a person with a dream
has a lot of thought.
Thought that's real
and thought that's not.
Screams, yells
Some bad and some good.
Falling, flying through the air
Yelling, but no sound,
Running, but not moved
Green men, blue men
You and me
Bad men and good men
Sad, but not felt
Hurt, but not touched.
Bad, but not punished
Punished, but not bad.

                 Chris Hales, 5th

A Dream

A Dream is like
A private heaven
Only for me,
A Dream is
Like all your
Thoughts chained
Together
A Dream is
Like a jungle
of thoughts,
Many things may
Happen in a
Dream.
A Dream
is the key to
Life,
A Dream may
Seem to last
Forever,
But may be
very short
indeed.

                 Peter Touborg, 4th

I dream about that I had big white wings on my
    back I flapped.
my wings and went up and up I went too far
and I almost touched the sun.
The sun said what are you doing so far in space
I said nothing really just looking around
the sun said what beautiful wings you have I must
    have them
I said no! you can't.
Why said the sun.
I said because if you take them from me I will
    float
along in space -- the sun said I got to have your
    wings
because I been here for millyins of years and I
    am getting
sick of it I said that's too bad
I think I will give you the wings and you can go
    somewhere
so I did give the sun my wings
and he went somewhere and I took his place with
    a shining face.

                 Larry, 4th

Old

Being old is kind of scary and lonesome
sometimes. My grandfather passed away
but he's in my mind. Our family thinks
that he's still in the house living with us,
in fact he is. We find his favorite cigars
downstairs in the basement where my
rabbit stays. Sometimes when our family
goes for a walk, we smell the cigar
and stop walking and say, "hi, grandfather,"
and we have dreams about him. And our family,
when we were in Texas and having fun, sometimes
when we heard him, we'd say hi, are all the
     people
we know up there fine?" and then we'd say bye.
                                        Rena Johnson

I dreamt that I was fooling around with the
     mirror
and I got really mad at something
cuz my mom called me to do something and I hit
     the mirror
and I stepped into the mirror
and I was in a whole different dimension
and it was where shadows of everybody were
my mother's twin and my father's twin
and when I met up with my own twin we had a
     giant battle
and I was running away and I decided
I could walk through the mirror again
and I tried to go through
and I couldn't fit through the mirror again
like I did when I got into the dimension
and all the other shadows teamed up with my
     twin
and they all started fighting and then
they jumped on me and I woke up
                                        Kent, 5th

FANTASY

Writing our daydreams is keeping track of our inner realities, not just letting them float in and out of our world. It means focusing in and paying attention to these realities, writing them down and speaking them out.

I am very much interested in the thin line between fantasy and reality in our lives. I bring in several poems for the children, and after reading IN MY OTHER LIFE by Sally Reynolds, I ask them about fantasy.

In My Other Life

The fireplace is growing crocuses
the snow is shrimp
my teacup a swan
the children are jasmine
lost past the hour of half
in my other life, hallucinations
will not open sausages of blood
nor let the mute gray wolves
follow

In my other life
seeds of apples are cranberries
apricots swell in transparent globes
lily tongue stamen lick the night

where I live
there are swaying beaches
a surf of flowers
lapislazuli horses lope

Pinecones petal me
in pungent rosin

I live on porches warmed
by blackbelly stoves
burning coal to roses

In my other life
my hide shakes rain as stars
                                        Sally Reynolds

Where is the poet's other life? What are the mute grey wolves and sausages of blood? Where do we travel when we begin to daydream? What are the specific names of our fantasies?

Trek

I wander
through seedless winters
I hike
through broken fixtures
plastic capsules insolvent dolls
and wrens called jenny.

I tip-toe
through sexton's sermons
televised fixed
bayonets I do
a slow breast stroke
through soft drinks
plucked bottle caps
I try all the tricks
before nightfall
I learn my craft
last of all
I sleep
Then my fingers
touch
what they want
the under-
sides of things
veins and filigree
tassles and glazes
rose arbor in the dusk
zebra scrimshaw one ebony mask

two tow-headed children
flickering on a distant beach
I dip my hands in
they come out
miraculously
dry

Elizabeth McKim

I read them the last part of *Alice in Wonderland* where the fantasy shifts between a dream and the real sounds of the meadow:

from *Alice in Wonderland*

. . . So she sat on, with closed eyes, and half believed herself in Wonderland, though she knew she had but to open them again and all would change to dull reality -- the grass would be only rustling in the wind, and the pool rippling to the waving of the reeds -- the rattling teacups would change to tinkling sheep bells, and the Queen's shrill cries to the voice of the shepherd boy -- and the sneeze of the baby, the shriek of the Gryphon, and all the other queer noises would change (she knew) to the confused clamor of the busy farmyard -- while the lowing of the cattle in the distance would take the place of the Mock Turtle's heavy sobs . . . . .

I ask the children to write about their fantasies. They should try to focus on "their other life" and record their daydreams or fantasies. And if they want to contrast this to their "real" lives, they might try that too. Many children won't admit they have fantasies, perhaps because they feel the fantasies are too private. One has to be sensitive to the group, its age and maturity. The way in which you would approach fantasy with junior high school students might be quite different from the way in which you would discuss it with elementary school children.

Two Lives

Now,
My life is real
I am me.
Things are the same.

Then,
I change.
I am anyone I care to be.
Things are different.
The room disappears.
I'm on the streets of Lochos, France.
I'm at the market
Talking fluent French
to my friends.
Chickens
hanging from the ceiling
of the butchers truck.
Cows' tongues draped over the sides.

Bang!
A door slams.
I'm interrupted.
Back to my room.

Cilla Smith, 6th

Shut your eyes because I'm going to take you to
    my land.
Here we are in my land, way above the clouds,
'Way above the heavens,
'Way up into space where it's my land.
In my land there is no pollution or dirty air,
No more cars go whizzing by,
No more Moms nagging you to do this or that,
No more cleaning up your room.
You get whatever you want, like junk food, and
    to stay up late.
You name it, and that's what it's like in my land.

                Joy Drachman, 6th

My special place is a cloud
Soft and pink
I lay down in the softness
Listen and think
In the background
I can hear COZ
And the sky is blue
As far as you can see
The sun is shining
Happy and bright
Other than this one
Not a cloud in sight
My special place is soft
Very soft and warm
It is the nicest place
I've been in
Since ever I was born.

                Jean Chambers, 6th

My Bedroom

My Bedroom turns into
a forest,
the things in it become
wild and fierce animals,
part of the floor becomes
a water hole for when
the animals get thirsty,
the ceiling becomes the
sky, the animals have homes
in the dirt and trees,
the light becomes the
sun, the animals walk around
doing nothing.

                Sheila MacKinnon, 6th

Noises

The noises become fish,
smoothly in the water they swim
Each noise is the bubble of a
    fish
A bubble holding precious
    secrets
and thoughts
A bubble which becomes an echo
    THE ECHO OF LIFE

                Shelby Hall, 6th

Before

Before you drift off into dreamland
Before going into unconsciousness
Before letting the mind lose control
Before letting the truth unload
        producing
        directing
        and starring in your own show
Before your spirit leaves you
Before going into a higher world
Before letting your future be told
Before painting your masterpiece
Before the romance
        the comedy
        the adventure
        the horror
You have to brush your teeth.

                Mali Lipchik, 8th

Poem for Judy

You milk your anguish into your poems
And I drink them, still warm, in rapture.
            *
Who are you to me?
            *
Are you my secret sister?
Have we walked on auburn pine needles together
among kind weak-sighted elves, or were they
    gnomes, or were they dwarves,
or were they people?
Have we braided the mane
of a sad sighing horse color of the dusk?
Have our steps echoed in the endless tomb of a
    monastery?
Was it us, two black monks, glued to the black
    damp walls,
listening, afraid of sound? . . .

Did we ever, ever-I wish!-pick bright red
    mushrooms
on a solemn mystic graveyard?
        . . . Silent motionless crows on
           black marble.
        Misty black marble-maybe
           fog, maybe tears . . .
Have we rode bareback bay Indian horses down
    the mountain,
onto the black cold beach of Ontario?
Was it us, pressing a copper coin against the frosty
    window,
breathing on it,
watching the Snow-Queen arrive on her mad
    white-furred horses?
        *

Was it you whose presence I sensed
entering a strange Japanese house
of unclear shadows on the clean grey and yellow
    silk?
Was it you who kissed me to be a poet, not know-
    ing my strength?
Was it you, who led me into the hen-coop of
    middle-class passion
and left me there?
        *

Throw off the cover! . . .
I no longer see you as an orange guitar,
wrapped in a doll's dress.
I no longer smell the Christmas tree.
You are back.
        Carrying the trophy-a handful of Adam's
           scales.
You are back,
        A woman who's tasted raw Solitude.

        Zoya Spivakovsky, at age 15

FREE ASSOCIATION AND STREAM OF CONSCIOUSNESS

What is free association? I ask the children one morning. "Being friends with anyone you like?" one boy says. Sounds great. But how about words. I'll say one and you say whatever pops into your mind, as quickly as possible.

We try it out. I say KNIFE. He says blood, meat, sharp, silver, glint, sun, water, ripple, edge, shore, weeds, rats, teeth, ice, crack, cut. We are leaping from word to word, from image to image

as a climber might do from rock to rock, not quite sure what lies ahead. We do not know where the association will take us, but the possibilities are exciting.

If you jump into the stream of your mind and just float along, feeling the direction of your movement, allowing yourself to change direction, beginning to keep track of your thoughts and feelings which appear and disappear, this is what we call free association, and poetry is, by nature, associative language. One image brings us to another; one word reminds and recalls. We are not always sure where these wrods will take us when we begin, and that is part of the excitement and possibility of poetry.

To convey this concept, I might ask the children to write for five minutes without stopping about what they are experiencing at this time, recording everything that comes into their heads, what they see in the room, what sounds they hear, whether their hand hurts from writing, the boy they are worried about, their sister who is mad at them, the smell of smoke from outside, the fact that nothing seems to be coming into their minds.

Witness

The wind, a smooth unbroken rush, reaches,
    subsides.
The faucet in the kitchen drips, apart. The cotton
    curtains
blow slowly in and out, filling with light. The
    sound of the
car engine on the street builds and retreats,
    echoing the
rise and fall of the wind. Everything in my space
    names me.
I rub my hand against the page of a book. That
    too has a
texture, makes a sound. I look out the window.
    The sun streams
across my book. I see the shadow of my hand,
    writing, crossing
the page. A plane goes by. I hear the engine. I do
    not see it.
I feel the vibration of someone in the building,
    moving across
the floor. The wind comes up again. A small pen-
    dant I have
hung at my window taps against the glass. I look

at my notebook.
My daughter has drawn a picture for me before
  she left to visit
her father. I miss her sharply.
  Elizabeth McKim

At the end of this exercise, some usually want to share these out loud. It is interesting to share this journey of our imagination, thoughts, and feelings. This exercise helps us not to censor before we write, which is necessary if honest poetry is going to be written. Editing material out is easy once it is written down, but it is hard to reveal the richness of our selves if we censor before we write.

Once I mistakenly suggested to some sixth graders that they could choose portions to edit out of all the "garbage" of their stream of consciousness writing. One girl replied, "but it's the garbage that makes it interesting."

Dreams, of course, do not censor and also go between what seems real and what seems strange. In *Leaping Poetry*, Robert Bly says . . ."children move back and forth between the known and unknown minds with a minimum of fear." We want to validate this ability, not ignore it or repress it. We want to make use of the richness it provides for us.

In a poem, the ability to leap from one image to another, to make exciting and unexpected connections between images or between words, has produced powerful poems which make a difference in our lives.

This Is

This is the earth.
This is a caterpillar on the earth.
This is the moon floating over the earth.
This is a lady dancing and falling asleep.
This is a rocket falling apart.
This is a lady making something.
This is a fat man.
His bed is falling apart.
This is a box with a ring in it.
Did the ring just fall out?
Where is it going?
It might be going to the center of the earth.
  Chris Martin, 2nd

The Waves Fly

The waves fly
Like so many birds.
The droplets
Shine.
The waves go up and the bird
Breaks.
A thousand hundred million tiny
Spiders
Fly through the air, each
Letting out a gleam.
The sun hits the spiders,
And they disappear.
Tiny firefalls fly.
They descend
Slowly,
A million turquoise gems,
Thousands of millions
Worth more than a real gem.
This gem is for all,
It is magic,
The magic of Uno,
God of Water,
Ever-continuing
Bird flying
Spider leaping
Fireball whizzing
Gem falling

Bid flying
Spider leaping
Fireball whizzing
Gem falling

Falling
Falling
Forever.

  Tara Kelly, 5th

110

Above, singer/songwriter Victor Cockburn demonstrates how musicians create lyrics for songs or use original poems to set to music.

Below, poet Etheridge Knight visits students to discuss the process of making poems.

Guest artists representing the various forms of expression can have a large impact on students. When children hear a range of voices in poetry or have a chance to experience the work of songwriters, dancers, and visual artists, they not only have models but, by sharing the quality work of practicing artists, have a taste of the excitement, vision, and subject matter unique to each artist.

Young poet Chrystal Donegan-Adade meets Pulitzer Prize winner Gwendolyn Brooks

Color

Can you tell me about the sky in a new way? The sky can be black or silver, or a rainbow, or green if you are daydreaming about summer in the middle of winter, or red if you want to pull it down in anger, or orange because you are so happy you want to reach up and embrace it, all of it. Colors have a lot to do with feelings. You might read _Hailstones and Halibut Bones_ together. Close your eyes and begin with one color. What images start flooding the darkness under your eyes? What sounds do you associate with that color? What feelings? Be the color. Talk to it. How is it dressed? Where might it live? Paint your world with it. The passages below are presented in the way I might talk with the children about color, using associative language and stream of consciousness writing to share the feeling of the dialogues between me and the students.

GREEN

Green. Who _are_ the green people? Green. Vert. Verde. Make up another word for green. What do you see when you think green? Maybe you see gold. Green and gold together. Summer, space, growing up, a worn down spot of grass behind your old house, a parade of green horses, a tall green man speaking in long green thoughts.

Let your mind flow with green. Water colors. What do you meet and mix with? Who are the enemies of green? Let green words and letters and green numbers appear. Green animals. If you met GREEN on the street what would he or she be like? What would she say? What would she wear?

What would her songs be like? Have you ever heard of a green poem? Seen a green bee? Is there a land of green dreams? What sounds like green? Grrr. reen. rain. grain, green rain cluster.

Try an acrostic. (Do one on the blackboard with the help of the children.)

Goodbye to you
Red Rabbit, I have chosen another, a certain
_   green_
Eagle, shining on flat grass, singing an
End to my sadness, my red tales. Now I sail with
_   giant_
New wings, practicing the span of my feathers.

Green

Salt water on the beach
thick grass in summer
astonished leaves in summer
pine needles in summer
limes in harvest
plants any time of year.
                    Bobby Boylan, 6th

BLUE

A blue mother? Blue stones, hundreds of blue stones drowsing in puddles, blue leopards in an African dusk, a blue skate, six blue melting snowmen. Blue is talking and having no one listen. Blue is just before I go to sleep. Blue is tomorrow walking to school. Yes. Blue is very skinny and talks in a soft voice and wears feathers. Blue is a stylish woman wearing a mask, and when she walks in blue silk I hear sss whshsh slip, whssh slip; I hear the sound of cold water going over smooth rocks, very high up. Yes, she lives in a blue forest, and she talks to herself and when she does she stops being blue. She loves foxes.

Blue, bay, leak, loon, mane, moon, moon stone, blue moon stone, blue stables in moonlight, blue stallions.

Blue

blue
as the wrinkled wall
paper of the elephant
heart

blue chambers
of mother-
blood

blue
life
magazines

stacked in
the entry way
of the old

apartment
on Fuller St.
blue kites

skitter
in the after-
noon light

Elizabeth McKim

Blue Cornucopia

Pick any blue sky-blue cerulean azure
cornflower periwinkle blue-eyed grass
blue bowl blue bell pick lapis lazuli
blue pool blue girl blue Chinese vase
or pink-blue chicory alias ragged sailor
or sapphire bluebottle fly indigo bunting
blue dragonfly or devil's darning needle
blue-green turquoise peacock blue spruce

blue verging on violet the fringed gentian
gray-blue blue bonfire smoke autumnal
haze blue hill blueberry distance
and darker blue storm-blue blue goose
ink ocean ultramarine pick winter
blue snow-shadows ice the blue star Vega.

Robert Francis

RED

What are your red feelings? What does red look like? What are the red sounds, letters, and numbers? What are the red animals? Tell me about the red land. Who does red fight with and what does he say when he fights? Fire, fruit, and vegetable, all red. Season of red. Red, rouge, *morado*. What happens in the stillness of red? Is red old or young? Red is an ancient man on a mountain shouting chants into the gorge below. Red is clenched. Red is locked up in a room inside a cave inside a battleship inside a red whale. Even the sea is red. Red minnows shining. Bloodstone, ruby, scarlet, orange, pink. How does red change?

Red

Red tastes like a red juicy apple
And the water red from the setting
      sun.
The beautiful red reminds me of
      love and heartbeats pounding.
The red berries smushing on side-
      walks
Red is also bad things like
The bright fire colors, orange
yellow and red, burning
down the inside of a beautiful
red brick house.
Red is when people are embarrassed
turning all rosy red.
When daddy pulled me in my
little red wagon and I
laughed so joyously.

Grace Gruenler, 6th

Red

at first
the red bird/raced
into the polar snows/streaked
the green mountain/swatted
the blue perimeter/ yes stained
the black permanently yes
the red bird fanned the sky
like a fire sign/and I laughed
at last.

                    Elizabeth McKim

BLACK

Noir. Black is the face of the black child, the black man, the black woman. Black is the bark of a tree after rain, black is the earth under snow, the warm center of the earth, black is the center of the eye, black is the night. Black, click, lake, luck, lack, black beaches under the hot sun, lick of licorice, black bear fur rubbed, black streets after the long days, blackberry, black fox running the hill, Blackfoot Indians, black ice in January.

Gold

and gold
        as daffo-
        dills down daddy's
        garden gleaming

and gold as
        dazed li-
        on eye-
        ing kite

        in late light
        spring falling
        corn flowers
        fill old
        lion-
        mouth

                    Elizabeth McKim

Listen to the other names for colors taken from the thesaurus: *white, snow-white, creamy, frosted, silvery ivory, ash-blond, blanched, black, ebony sable, ink, pepper and salt, dune, dove-colored, dappled, nut-brown, seal, mahogany, fawn, tan, bronze, terra cotta, maroon, russett, roan, sorrel, henna, auburn, hazel, rust, scarlet, cardinal, cerise, salmon, magenta, damask, coral, chestnut, sea-aquamarine, emerald, lemon, saffron, citron, amethyst, plum, lilac, azure, indigo, electric, midnight, sapphire, royal blue.*

What Color Is Black?

black is the color of
my little brother's mind
the grey streaks
in my mother's hair
black is the color of
my yellow cousin's smile
the scars upon my
neighbor's wrinkled face.
The color of
the blood we lose
the color of our eyes
is black.
our love of self
of others
brothers sisters
people of a thousand
shades of black
all one.
black is the color of
the feeling that we share
the love we must express
the color of our strength
is black.

                    Barbara Mahone

Memories

What we remember from yesterday or many years ago provides us with important material for our poems. Our storehouse of memories affects who we are as people. Some of the memories that stay with us are clear images in our minds: the games we played with a grandfather on the lawn, the first day of school, the time we fell out of a tree and broke a leg, having tonsils out in the hospital, the loss of a friend.

These are real and honest experiences, and poems which are made from this material are easy for others to appreciate. Some of us have memories of events which we believe we experienced, but they are really memories of stories or myths told to us by parents or grandparents. These memories are part of our inheritance, our family heirlooms.

I Ask My Mother to Sing

She begins, and my grandmother joins her.
Mother and daughter sing like young girls.
If my father were alive, he would play
his accordian and sway like a boat.

I've never been in Peking or the Summer Palace
nor stood on the great Stone Boat to watch
the rain begin on Kuen Ming Lake, the picnickers
running away in the grass.

But I love to hear it sung;
how the waterlilies fill with rain until
they overturn, spilling water into water,
then rock back, and fill with more.

Both women have begun to cry,
But neither stops her song.

Li -Young Lee

We discuss how the poet made this memory come alive by using his senses and the stories he was told about the country he came from. He paints a picture with words for himself and the reader.

We begin to share some of our important memories. I try to suggest the range of memories we carry with us so children can spin back through a variety of their own. When they begin to write, I ask the children to focus on describing a memory in as much detail as possible, making up specifics when they don't remember. What were their feelings at the time of the incident?

This kind of writing session may bring up events for children that can be painful. A fourth grade boy recalled the day his grandfather died. He was intent on writing about this, even though he began crying in the process and needed to finish his writing in a private corner near an adult. We do not have to avoid emotional material, just be sensitive to the individual situations of each child, providing support and understanding for children who are anxious to work with these personal sources. I respect children who do not want to share these poems with others; however, I am surprised by how often they do want to read them to the class despite their revealing or even painful aspects. Poems like this are extremely important for the development of an atmosphere of trust among students and teachers. The poems encourage children to use real life situations in their expressive work.

116

EXAMPLES BY STUDENTS:

Ice Skating

I glide on the ice
I feel cold and warm at the same time
I start to topple like a bowling pin
My hands won't move to catch me
I cry to my father to help me
I see blood as red as a ruby
Falling on the ice
I cry, I cry
What is this?
Someone has brought my father
I hear talk of stitches
I say, "No, no!"
My father takes me to the hospital
I get interviewed!
I feel important
I get asked questions like "Did you pass out?"
I think, "don't ask such silly questions"
I go into a room and sit on a bed
A nurse comes in with a needle
"Oh, no," I say, " a shot!"
I get my stitches
It tickles
It is amazing!
I live.

Saamra Rosa Mekuria-Grillo, 4th

These Children I Love

Waaa!
Shhhh!
The smell of sweet air,
baby powder.
The feelings of sadness and happiness
I walk into the spot,
where Jamie first crawled into my
hands.
This was the spot I love most,
Where I picked up Alyson,
where Megan cried
and where I met William,
Right here.
The spot where I sang Maya to sleep.
Where Judith talked,
where Alyson first walked to me,
and we all clapped.
The place by the swing,
this place I love most!

Nikki Schall, 5th

This poem was written by Sandra about her late grandmother in Spain.

Un Recuerdo

En el fondo de su casa vive,
su espíritu en el silencio
con sus cosas y utensilios
en la oscura eternidad.
En la ventana,
sus vestidos vuelan sin cesar,
pero no se escapan no.
Se retienen,
no se quieren ir,
su estado los detiene
parece que recuerdan a mi abuela
  alegre, tradicional,
y su boca, chiquita como una almendra,
  sus ojos, negros como la más oscura noche,
brillan sin cesar.
Con sus manos
trabajando sin cesar
trabajó contenta hasta su muerte.
Me contaron que cogió una tigresa y una serpiente.
La tigresa, amarilla como el sol con la noche
y la serpiente larga y gruesa.
Me gustaría haber estado allá, haber sido ella.
Tuvo hijos, todos fieles a su madre que fué su maestra.
Algunas veces, me arrepiento de haber nacido tan
pronto, pero no fué mi culpa.

La vida es así: INJUSTA.

Sandra Calderón Charles, 6th

A Memory

In the back of her house lives
her spirit in silence with her belongings
in the eternal darkness.
In the window, her clothes float in the breeze
but they can't escape, no.
They are trapped,
They don't want to leave.
And it seems as though they
remember my grandmother,
her happy traditional ways,
her mouth, small like an almond,
her eyes, black, like the darkest night
shining ceaselessly.
Her hands always working,
working contentedly until her death.
They told me that she caught a tigress and a serpent.
The tigress, yellow like the sun with the night,
and the serpent heavy and thick.
I would like to have been there, to have been her.
She had sons, all faithful to their mother,
their teacher.
Sometimes I regret having been born so recently,
but the fault is not with me.
Life is that way: UNJUST!

translated by Maria Marrero

New Year

This is the old way,
the whole clan gathered,
the rice steaming over the charcoal.
the women in the room, talking,
a layer of potato starch on the table.

This is the old way, the father watching
*   his son lift the mallet,*
pound the rice, pound mochi,
the children watching or playing,
the run of the dough to the women,
the rolling of the round cakes.

This is the old way,
eating ozoni, new year's soup:
mochi for longevity,
daikon, long white radish
rooted firmly like families;
eating burdock, also deeply rooted,
fish for general good luck,
the lotus root, wheel of life.

This is the old way, setting off firecrackers
to drive away evil spirits,
leaving the driveways red for good fortune.

The new year arrives,
deaf, smelling of gunpowder.

Gail N. Harada

118

Changes

In our lives, we are always undergoing change. As babies, we learn to crawl, then walk. We learn to make sounds, then talk. The day we arrive at school for the first time is a tremendous change. We respond to changes in the seasons and changes in the environment. We undergo emotional change when friends move away, when a parent leaves home, when we change schools, or visit a strange country. In poetry, we acknowledge these changes and give them the importance they deserve.

Things Happen

in flashes
forsythia streams
from gold into green
the apple trees jag
into bloom for a day
a child speaks

a child says NO
a brother is born
as sudden as night
on the equator

we live in the instant
of lightning
bugs pulsing in darkness
sparking from thickets

sudden as fire
blooming on branches
we burn
until dawn.

Judith Steinbergh

I ask the children to think back over their lives and see if they can pick out an event which changed them significantly, something that has stayed an important memory. Or they might review how their bodies and minds respond to cyclical changes such as the seasons or to trips between country and city or to the atmosphere of day and how it differs from night.

EXAMPLES BY STUDENTS:

My Grandfather

Those light blue eyes that once
sparkled with light were now
dull.
The lively grandfather that once
jumped and played with me
was now as still as the night.
The joking man was now still
and serious.
There he lay in the coffin
dead.
As we all joined hands,
The man recited a prayer.
He said something about grandpa
being under the daisies.
I was five when he died.
I believed he was under the daisies
Up in heaven
Where he belonged.

Joscelyn Jurich, 4th

Good-Bye!

The last day,
The last time,
Into the empty house
my friend and I walked:
hand in hand.
If I said anything,
It would echo back to me.
I could not,
I would not,
say good-bye.

Those times we had once together.
Those times we had once shared
Were now over.
The sun was going down
and the room was growing dark.
My friend and I stood still.

Then a small hand
touched my shoulder.
And a tear wet my hand.
For both of us knew it was over
as we stood there being still.
The blaring sound of a horn
made her stand up and
as she walked out
she touched me
and said in a quiet
soothing voice
Good-Bye.
I stood there
until the car was out of sight.
Then
suddenly
I wanted to see her again.
I wanted to hold her hand
and say
Good-Bye
I hadn't even said
Good-Bye.

                              Melissa Moake, 4th

Death

A person dies
and leaves,
but never really leaves,
they disappear from sight
but their remembrance
still lingers on.

She passed on, a year ago
and changed my life, very so.

no cousin, no beach!
no fridays of love
that were in my life
a year ago.

                              Randy Tye, 7th

The Golden Chain (just before it blooms),

I'm plain now, an old rag tree.
Now I'm normal, any old plant,
but I conceal something deep inside me,
During spring, I won't bloom,
but soon oh so soon my ugly buds
All spiny and sticky will grow,
My seeds will bloom into a golden silk,
Now no ragwood will be me,
Golden grapes all shiny in a row,
Husbands pick me for their wives,
Children like to throw me,
I can be a golden grenade,
Or a strip of sunshine hanging in glee,
Me, oh me, soon beautiful me!

                              Eric Marshall, 6th

Friend

My friend, he is gone now.
I fear he will not come back
to live here.
I long for him.
I am lonely.
I can still remember when we played
When he would have me over one day
and I would have him over the next.
When we talked at the playground
about our dreams.
When he would come over and we would
play imaginative games.
But them he left to some far away place.
I fear he will never come back
to live here.

                              Chris King, 6th

The Becoming

of a blossom,
getting bigger and stronger,
feeling new veins and seeds moving through me.
I am an apple, a full happy apple,
swinging on my branches.
I know something's going to happen
though, something
new and exciting.
I can feel it in my stem.

I knew it.
Here is something, something
strong clasping on me,
sweaty tentacles
gripping grabbing pulling.
I knew something was going to happen
But why this?
Why me?
Here I am
Crowded and jumbled around many apples
in a basket.
Some may be friends or even relatives.
I'd love to talk and ask questions:
Where am I?
Who are those things?
What's happening?
I wish I could go back
to the quietness of my tree.
And again I am here
Puzzled and smothered, questioning.
I am getting used to surprises,
But I still question.
Why me?
I am lying here, being smothered
by the many unknown things
on top of me.
The string of the bag
burns into my skin,
while my heart wonders.
I never knew life
Could be so hard.

Wow! This is a strange sensation,
part of my being cut off
mangled in between
hard sharp teeth,
and moved around by a hard scratchy tongue.
Is life coming to an end?
What is happening?
. . . now everything is peaceful.

I am flying through the air
knowing that all my torture
is over. I mean
it must be!
My life is always full
of questions.
I don't know what to do.
Is it possible
for an apple to commit suicide?
I am being sucked into the ground.
I try to pull off the dark earth,
try to stay free.
But after a while of struggling
I just let the earth cover me,
smother me.
Though now, I feel peaceful,
happy. I must let
whatever is coming, come.
I am lying here,
feeling something new,
my body is tingling with some new
unexpected surprise. I think
I know deep inside,
but I just can not reach it.
I can feel it now,
a new attachment to my body.
I peek out, scared but excited,
and there it is!
A branch, that I,
with only myself, have produced!
And now, here I am, a baby tree!
Tired but strong.
I've just had the most incredible
feeling. I have been transformed
from apple to tree,
a new beginning, a new life!
I am pretty now!
Big, gorgeous, too big
to be hurt, just happy!
I am growing blossoms now.
Popping out from my luscious branches.
The beginnings of new lives.
Hopefully better than mine.
I've done it. With hours of hard work
I finally got what I wanted.
Hundreds of miniature macs,
happy and free, ready
to go into the world.
My life has been torture.
But it has been worth it.
Yes worth it.

Jenifer McKim

Loneliness

Whish, Whish, air blows on my face
Everybody ignores me
I feel as if the day has taken over the night
I feel as if I am being enclosed in a jar
and kids don't like me
The jar is very small
And so am I
I'm not a big thing in this world, just small
My voice grows tiny, like a mouse
My feelings are the same, hurt and shallow
Once I get my hopes up I can break the jar
and my voice is strong
My heart is no longer weak, I'm strong.

                              Mona Fergus, 5th

Gone Except Memories (in memory of Ray)

Kindly man,
few knew him well,
most called him solitary,
for his smiles said more than his words.

He roamed the streets and back alleys,
Shaggy clothes and unshaved face,
Kindly man seemed immortal
until one day he wasn't there.

He wasn't seen for weeks on end,
his presence sorrily missed.
But to this day he still remains,
Gone except memories.

                              Sarah Larysz, 5th

122

Conflict

This is a session I usually reserve until I have worked with students for a while with other themes and processes.

Conflict and tension are a real part of life, and therefore of poetry. This lesson is focused on trying to make us open to these conflicts and finding verbal means of expressing them, and therefore of changing and transcending them. Perhaps it is a question of accepting these conflicts, and allowing them a voice and a substance within the poem. The children will know what you are talking about: love and hate inextricably mixed, night and day, elephant and ant, waking and sleeping. It touches deeply their own experience. They have all had the experience of loving someone and yet getting so angry they wanted to harm him or her. This lesson has to do with wishes and fears, present and past, questions and answers, and the paradox that one answer usually leads to another question, and on and on.

The poems will find shapes and forms. Perhaps one line for one voice and one line for another. [Perhaps the conflict is told by an outside observer. Perhaps there will be one stanza for one voice or attitude and another stanza for the other.] The poems may deal with polarities, opposites, tension and release. A fence being built and a fence being torn down. Ask students to consider the rhythms of life, the process that is at work in us and in the world we live in.

If the children talk about peace and war, love or hate, be sure they relate it to what they know and have experienced. This is a session that can bring up deep angers and frustration. For that reason, we must be very sensitive to what children are saying. With sensitivity, this exercise may be used to work with classroom conflicts.

No I Won't

*No I won't go to the market to
    get a gallon of milk
No I won't go to the post office to
    get the mail
No I won't go down the street to
    get my little brother
They send me here they send me
    there they send me all around
the square WHAT SHOULD I DO!
I'll tell them to go to the
    market to get a gallon of milk
I'll tell them to go to the post-
    office to get the mail
I'll tell them to get my little
    brother.
I'll send them here I'll send
    them there I'll send them all
around the square. I'll tell
them now Good Bye.*

Nancy, 6th

A Feisty Creature

I am a young feisty little creature.
I get upset when I'm told that I will not
be allowed to do something.
I have sensitive feelings,
but I can cause internal pain in others.
I used to have ridiculous fears,
but soon overcame them.
I try not to judge people from their appearances.
When I go to different places,
sometimes people stare at me
because I have more carotene in my skin.
This upsets me, but I sometimes do it also.
I want to try to get out of this habit
so that I can be a better person.
This is why I came here,
so I could learn about people
who have handicaps and people who've had
different experiences than myself.

Deanna Brannon, 8th

Perfection

I would like
to be perfect. I would like
to have black hair. I would like
to weigh fifty pounds. My skin
will always be tan, and I will
never be sallow. My dress is
always stylish and clean. I look
and feel graceful. I would be
clean all the time and my nails
would always be short.
Everyone would like me.
I would be smart. My eyes
would be turquoise.
I would be very kind.

Girl, 5th

The Pest

He goes through my things
as if he has just found a treasure box
finding out what is in it,
for he is the brother
the pest.
Teases me 'til I'm a volcano
ready to blow up
for he is the brother
the teaser.
Proud of the trouble he makes
like a horse that has just won a race
proud
for he is the brother.
Like an ant who is always
crawling up your arm
a pain
for he is the brother
annoying,
But if you're nice
he is a kitten curled up
in your arm purring,
the sweet
for he is the brother.
He will sleep on the couch
or the bed
for he is the brother
the tired one.
He can be many things
The pest
The teaser
The proud
And the pain
He is the sweet
The tired one
He is many things
For he is the brother.
He is the pest.

Rebecca, 5th grade

Fable

Once not long ago there was a brother and a sister
      who loved to fight.
They fought like two mice over a piece of cheese.
They fought like two geese over a sprinkle of
      seeds.
They fought like two sharks, like two crabs, like
      two barracudas.
He could not keep his foot to himself.
She could not keep her nails to herself.
They fought like two spiders over a fly.
They fought like two asteroids over the sky.
They fought like two oceans over a beach, roaring
      and spitting
grinding shells up, tearing rocks away, wrenching
      kelp from its roots.
They fought like two volcanos over a peak,
      burning whole forests
of redwoods, trees that had spent hundreds of
      years getting as thick as they were.
They fought like two glaciers over who was
      melting more slowly.
They fought like two suns over who could attract
      more planets.
They fought like two mosquitoes over a drop of
      blood.
They fought like two Corvettes on a narrow road.
She could not think of a sweet thing to say to him
He could not think of a pleasant word to say to
      her.
From the crack of dawn until the last bitter ex-
      change before they fell
into bed, they tossed names back and forth like a
      hot potato: names like
numbskull whatever that is and stupid and dope-
      head and words too bad to even
put into a poem by a grown-up, they forgot the
      real name of the other
Oh said the mother this is unacceptable behavior,
      this is intolerable noise,
if you don't stop you can't have dessert, if you
      don't stop you'll go
to your rooms, if you don't stop I'll spank you
      both
But she'd taken his money and he'd taken her
      market and she'd taken his capgun
and he'd taken her bear and she was going to

throw her apple at him and he
was going to dump her cereal on her
Oh said the mother if you don't stop I'm not sure
      I can be a mother another minute

But they didn't hear her, she said her best friend
      had two wagons and he said
she lied and she said she didn't and he said she did
      and
Oh the mother said I'm going to count to three
      and from then on we will only
say pleasant things to each other, one, two, three
But he insisted on sitting on her chair and she in-
      sisted on using his blue cup
and she refused to eat what he wanted for dinner
      and he refused to wash his
hands before dinner even though anyone could
      see he'd painted his fingers
with markers and made mudpies all afternoon not
      to mention other unmentionable things
unmentionable things
If we can't work things out said the mother we
      might not be able to live together
But she wanted him to sleep in her room with all
      the lights on and he wanted
to sleep in his own room with all the lights out
      and his eyes open besides and he
wanted a story and she didn't want that one, she
      wanted her back rubbed and
a different story and not rubbed in that place but
      another place further down
and he wanted to know why the mother was
      spending longer with her than with
him and she wanted to know what words the
      mother had said to him that she might
not have whispered to her
Now the mother was crying.
Why? they wanted to know. What could possibly
      be wrong? They both loved her so much.
Only he loved her more that she did. No she loved
      the mother more, hadn't she made
all those valentines with glitter, but hadn't he
written her poems?

                              Judith Steinbergh

Finding the tension between objects in nature–fire and water, ocean and sand, wind and rock, can make a powerful statement in poetry.

Tree versus Wind

Wind   *I can blow you down*
I am better than you.

Tree   *I can not be blown down*
I am better than you.

Wind   *I am more powerful*
I can blow on you and make you sway.

Tree   *I am wise, my roots reach deep*
in the ground and hold me steady.

Wind   *I am free to go where I want,*
I'm not bogged down to stay in one
place for my life..

Tree   *I am tall and beautiful*
with many arms that reach far out.

Wind   *I am fearless, I wander*
all over destroying what
I don't like, I cannot be stopped.
I toss planes around
like a tennis ball. I show no
mercy for kites or model planes.

Tree   *I am brave, I stand up tall*
to any danger that comes.
I do not wander away
from everything. You do.

Wind   *You fall down when the lumberjacks*
come, and you lose your leaves
in the winter and shake from the cold.

Tree   *I provide a home for many animals*
in winter and summer and when the
                    lumberjack
comes I will provide heat for people.
When he comes I stand tall and proud
until his mighty ax strikes me.

Wind   *Then I will watch in glory*
for here he comes with his mighty ax.
Now you will fall and I will be the best.
                   Jason Labelle, 6th

The following are some ideas for creating a poem of dialogue which might involve conflicts:

POEM OF YOU AND ME
POEM OF SOMEBODY AND NOBODY
POEM OF TERRIBLE ME AND PERFECT ME
POEM OF BABY ME AND GROWN UP ME
POEM OF LOVE AND HATE
POEM OF FIRE AND ICE
POEM OF TWO BRAINS
POEM OF ME AND MY SHADOW
POEM OF MY MOUTH AND MY BODY
POEM OF YES AND NO
POEM OF A FIGHT
POEM OF SPRING AND WINTER
POEM OF THE ANT AND THE ELEPHANT
POEM OF OUTSIDE AND INSIDE
POEM OF SPRING AND WINTER
POEM OF THE BOY AND THE GIRL
POEM OF THE BROTHER AND THE SISTER
POEM ABOUT SOMETHING I WISH WOULD
    HAPPEN AND SOMETHING I HOPE WILL
    NEVER HAPPEN
POEM OF BEING SCARED AND BEING
    BRAVE
POEM OF NIGHT AND DAY
POEM OF GOING AND COMING
POEM OF WAKING AND DREAMING

Forms

This section is going to be brief. Many teachers feel comfortable introducing simple forms of poetry to children and will do that from time to time throughout the year. Acrostics, haiku, tanka, cinquaine, diamante, alphabet poems are all forms which can provide children with just enough structure to allow them to express themselves freely.

I recommend the *Teachers and Writers Handbook of Poetic Forms*, edited by Ron Padgett, which clearly describes many poetic forms and includes examples and exercises for most of them. Acrostics and haiku often work with second and third graders; cinquaines, diamantes, and pantoums are appropriate for third through fifth or sixth. The blues form of lyrics, rap, and quatrains or couplets are challenging for fourth graders and older. And with students in eighth grade who have had some experience with poetry, it is fun to be able to recognize and to try writing a sonnet or a villanelle.

It is important for children to see rhyming poetry as only one of many kinds of poetry so their expectation of what a poem should be does not hamper their own expression. Here is a quick review of several forms with examples of each.

ACROSTICS

I ask the children what is special about this poem. When they guess it, they can't wait to begin. They do their own names, their friends' names, and then seasons, colors, and feelings.

Jellyfish
Undulating
Deep
In *the purple sea*
Their
Hearts *are everything.*

Rain

   The **R**ain
     is **A** song
        In my ear
   It is **N**ice
  A big **D**rop can
   be a **R**iddle in my ear
If you **O**pened the rain
    dro**P** there might be a poem.

                    Bryan Roderick, 2nd

Many *pink*
Ostriches *were*
Running *and strutting*
Restless *and yearning to be*
Independent *and free, they*
Slowly *are dying, we*
Scare *them away*
Even *now we still take their*
Young *and cage them into zoos*
              Karen Morrissey, 7th

HAIKU

Making jazz swing
in seventeen syllables ain't
no square poet's job.

Etheridge Knight

Haiku is a Japanese form of poetry. On one level it is usually about nature (the seasons, the sun and moon, rain and snow, animals and insects); on another level it is about self-revelation. The masters of haiku studied Zen for many years before they felt equipped to write a true haiku. I recommend borrowing a few books of haiku and reading *Haiku: The Mood of the Earth* by Ann Atwood, who speaks about the historical and spiritual basis of haiku in a simple way.

Haiku is a syllabic form (it doesn't rhyme) and in Japanese, the first and third lines have 5 syllables while the second line has 7 syllables. The idea is to present a vivid image in the first two lines and then make a surprise connection to something else in the third. You can break a sentence in the middle of a line. When the children are familiar with the form and have heard and tried a few, I ask them to write a series of haiku about something in nature: the four seasons, day and night, birth, life, and death. We then rewrite these in small booklets illustrating them with drawings or quick watercolors.

Haiku Seasonal Cycle

The lilies open
To announce a new season
Snow rabbits change hue.

The fox finds freedom
Heat waves rise off the moths' wings
The goldfish all swim.

Sharp, crisp winds blowing
Frost forms on the spider web
The animals hide.

The world is white now
Flaky snow from flaky clouds
Look forward to spring.

Charlton Pettus, 5th

Haiku Life Cycle

My eyes are open
I see my sisters and folks,
dogs, I hope they are mine.

Playing with my friends
the day is done for now, bye.
I rest in my bed.

My eyes are closed now.
God is coming for me now.
Goodbye forever.

Cindy Murphy, 5th

Haiku: The Seasons

the moon full and bright
shining on the fallen snow
like melted silver

green in the meadow
life awakes, yawns and stretches
water runs away

hundreds of birds, oh
shining in my sycamore
a cool summer breeze

mouse small, squeak quiet
the leafy whistling wind
days scurry away

Colin Steele, 5th

Big tree big tree
It is spring now it is time
To open up the leaves.

Shawn Hanigan, 2nd

The flower goes in
And out And that's life
And that's good!

Rachel DeFea, 2nd

A caterpillar oozed
It oozed through the grass
It oozed until it died.

David Ayer, 2nd

CINQUAINE

This form is also a syllabic form and has 5 lines with the following numbers of syllables: 2, 4, 6, 8, 2.

Mother
was squeamish at
the thought of blood, and soon
I learned to dig out my splinters
alone.

Mary Hazard

Vermont, Late October

After
blood of maple
had spilled on the cold ground,
dull copper beech, bleached bones of birch
remained.

Mary Hazard

Some children confuse counting syllables with counting words. You can help clear this up by making a communal poem, with different students suggesting every new line.

DIAMANTE

This is sometimes called a "Kite" poem as it often ends up shaped like a kite. It has the following structure.

line 1.   one noun
line 2.   two adjectives modifying it
line 3.   three verbs describing it
line 4.   four nouns, images associated with it
line 5.   three verbs modifying the last noun
line 6.   two adjectives describing the last noun
line 7.   the opposite of the first noun

Example:

ice
jagged, bluish
pointing, dripping, pricking
claws, teeth, dragon, breath
burning, searing, killing,
hot, brilliant
fire

Atoms
small, electricity,
exploding, skilling, helping,
Photons, Protons, Neutrons, Electrons,
destroying, lighting, powering
powerful, forceful,
nothingness

Paul Oreto, 3rd

A pantoum is based on repeating the second and fourth lines of each stanza as the first and third lines of each succeeding stanza. Leah wrote this under the guidance of her teacher Jack DeLong.

Sisters, A Pantoum

When I was born you were there
With dancing eyes singing hello.
Baby Bozo and the Little Tooth Fairy
Celebrating all my special days.

With dancing eyes singing hello
I learned my cartwheels at your side.
Celebrating all my special days
with you made me feel more special.

I learned my cartwheels at your side.
Sisters are friends. Laughing, singing and playing
with you made me feel more special.
I will see you wherever you are.

Sisters are friends. Laughing, singing, and playing.
We are together, forever, whispering secrets.
I will see you wherever you are.
You are my sister. What could be better?

Leah Tuckman, 3rd

Who Am I?

You may have noticed in reading this book that I am constantly asking questions. Who are you? Who am I? Poetry is, as I perceive it, the process of asking essential questions and trying to answer them through the vehicle of the poem.

Who Am I?

I can walk on the stars
And sleep in the clouds
I am the magician of thought
I can do anything
I can see the earth spinning
I hear the trees growing
I taste the starlight
I smell the universe
I feel the thoughts of men
I can save, renew, and revive.

Charlton Pettus, 5th

All the sources we draw on for our writing contain in them the question: *Who Am I? Who Am I* is determined by all the past experiences of our lives, and all our lives we move towards a greater understanding of this question. All poems confront this question either directly or indirectly. Even if the poem is about someone or something else, we are learning something about the poet by seeing the subject of the poem through the poet's eye.

Each of the previous exercises brings us further along this journey. Writing about ourselves using a mask or persona, or exploring how we respond to the world through all of our senses, or drawing upon our memories, dreams and fantasies, or confronting conflict and change in our lives, all help us define *Who We Are* to ourselves and to our friends.

What do we really look like? Could we describe ourselves with any precision to a stranger over the phone? How do we differ from our best friend? From our blood relatives? And even more importantly, how do we think that the image other people have of us differs from what we are really like inside?

We read Eloise Greenfield's poem, "By Myself," from *Honey, I Love* and Felice Holman's "Who Am I?" from *These Small Stones* (Farber and Livingston.)

What I Can Be

When I look in the mirror, I'm me..
When I close my eyes, I'm a famous explorer,
A lion tamer, I can hear the lions roar,
I'm a tight rope walker, a fast talker.
I'm as sly as a fox,
as square as a box,
I'm so fast I'd beat a train on the tracks,
I open my eyes,
I'm me! that's the best thing
there is to be.

Latoya, 4th

Sometimes I read this poem by Astrid. I ask the children to think about why she used the "image" of "a closed door" in this poem about herself.

...sed Door

...m filled with shyness
...at is all locked up.
My feelings are locked
in a big big chest.
With my own key
I open it up.
I am the only one who
can look through my feelings.
When I open my door, everbody
can tell I'm shy.

Astrid Alvarez, 5th

What image can they suggest for a person with a hot temper? "A volcano?" "A chili pepper?" What image can they suggest for a person who is very calm? "A mirror?" "A cool pond?" What are some images they can think of which might describe what they are like? I might ask them to write a poem using at least three of these images to describe their own personalities and strengths.

If You Want to Know Who I Am

If you want to know who I am
I'll yell it as loud as I can
I am as loud as the wind howling in a hurricane
I am like the big black clouds that look so loud
I am so loud
I am like a hot pink dress in a white room.

If you want to know who I am
I'll yell it as loud as I can
I like to be alone like a question mark
at the end of a question
I'm as alone as a tire on a unicycle.

If you want to know who I am
I'll yell it as loud as I can
I'm as sociable as a tree
starting to grow in a forest
I'm as sociable as a pony
who likes to neigh.

If you want to know who I am
I'll yell it as loud as I can
I'm a quiet little girl
as quiet as a flower on a sunny day
as quiet as a tree when the wind
is not whistling through me.

If you want to know who I am
I'll yell it as loud as I can
I am myself, and no one else
and that's who I am.

Kirsten Landry, 6th

Poema Jessica

Niña de cabellos negros
Sonrisa amigable,
risas que vuelan
por todo el mundo,
Jessica amiga
con sonrisa de
ruiseñar con voz
baja y ronca.

Que niña que
tiene una risa
que vuela y vuela
hasta que vaga y vaga
hasta que llega a una
persona. Jessica es
una niña que
sueña y sueña
con las risa.

Girl with black hair
Friendly smile
laughter that flies
all over the world.
Jessica, friendly
with a nightingale's
smile with a voice
low and hoarse.

What a girl who
has a laughter
that flies and flies,
it roams and roams
until it reaches a
person. Jessica is
a girl who
dreams and dreams
with laughter.

Jessica Paulina, 5th

At other times, I ask my students to ask themselves: "Who Am I?" They should give as many answers as possible and when they get stuck, ask themselves the same question again. I urge my students to write more than they think they need and choose the sections that please them most.

Who Am I?

Who am I, am I a hawk who likes to talk
and share with friends?

Who am I, am I a horse
who likes to neigh and play,
when I want to I fade away
and come back another day?

Who am I, am I a tornado
with the power of winds,
and when I feel mad, I feel
sad and wipe the village out?

Who am I, am I a fish who loves to swim
and flip with my fins and swim away?

Who am I, am I a star that shines very bright
all day and night? I am a star
that's happy, I want to shine, come on sun,
make it snappy.

Or am I a regular boy
who loves his family and friends
and loves to play, tell me!
Tell me! Tell me before
another day.

C. Martin, 5th

By Myself

When I'm by myself
and I close my
eyes very gently
to think ...
am I like cinnamon
on top of pie...

or am I spice
mixed up in the
mixture of french toast...

or am I sugar
on top of frosted flakes...

or am I peaches with the
distinguishing look...
or am I a pop-tart popping
up in unexpected places...

or am I a pencil
that constantly
needs to be sharpened
with more knowledge...

or am I a
spray pump
that is spraying out with more
answers to your questions...

or am I just me,
plain old me

Please tell me,
Oh please tell,
me who am I...

Nefertiti F., 5th

134

I often ask the children to draw self-portraits, drawing their whole bodies involved in a favorite activity, or just their faces, but filling the whole page. They might need to look in a mirror to remember the details of their faces or ask a friend for help. Rudy, from Teresa Berry's Spanish bi-lingual fifth grade wrote this poem in English.

Myself

I like myself because my eyes are dark as the night,
I like my hair because it's soft as fur.
And I behave like my friend, sometimes
I behave bad like a ferocious lion
and sometimes I behave good as a Angel.

I am great at running, I could run as fast
as a cheetah and I'm good at basketball.
I could play like Michael Jordan.

And if I could, I'd change the world into peace
and to love each other.

I like myself because God made me like I am
and I love God.

Rudy DeLeón, 5th

Me

I belong at the beach under the sun
but I glide on ice quickly and quietly,
I belong alone, reading
but I help out mothers,
I belong on my bed with my mind going wild,
but I sit at a party being quiet,
I belong balancing on a thin wire,
but I always watch out.
I belong with a chipmunk
but I sing with the Blue Jay.
When I grow up, I'd love to skate,
gliding, twirling, balancing.
I belong cuddling up with my mom,
then I sleep all night.

Karly Moore, 3rd

Me

I'm different from everybody else.
I'm an entertainer.
I'm a little shy.
But I get by.
I like to tap
day by day.
I grow and grow
night by night.
I sleep,
I dream,
of my best friends,
my talent, and me.

Sam Simon, 4th

Gifts

We listen to the voices of these children, introspective, searching, and profound, and it becomes clearer why poetry has a place in the classroom and in our lives. We owe it to each other and to our students to provide the space and time for this voice and to listen.

Nature's Way

In the gentle quiet,
I am understood,
I sit by a birch tree,
crying softly as a bird flies high above,
wondering what that bird is thinking,
but still, I am crying,
only to be interrupted by the dark
that falls upon me.

I am not scared, only touched
by darkness and its bewildering strangeness,
I think to myself: the changing of time,
seconds go by, then minutes, only to be
followed by hours, days, weeks, and
months, time, there is not enough of it.

For we live only 70 years on this planet,
make the most of it, look into nature,
see what life and its meanings have,
let emotions flow like the soft
gentle waves of the sea,
see how peaceful a forest is,
the trees swaying in the wind,

There is absolute quiet again,
and I cry, wondering why.

                    Gary Shurgin, 7th

The Music Box

I am music
I am life
I am the rising sun
the laughter of a baby boy or girl
*   with tiny curls.*
I am the singing of fairies so sweet
I am the melody
I am the song!

                    Jessica Field, 5th

I will sing and the clay will come into my hands.
I will make it the best pot in the world.
It will be the colors of the rainbow
and who ever touches it will be well again.
The horse on the pot is powerful.
It will come alive and it will be
the most beautiful horse in the world.
It will be as tall as a tree and strong as an ox.
I will sing and the clay will come into my hands.

                    Jeanne Williams, 4th

Emerging

The shine,
The yellow,
The golden
is rising
Can this be
The beginning?
My shining
My glow
My green
sight
so slowly
it opens
and buds into
a spotted flower.

I rise
my limbs
they open
and the dried skin peels
and reveals
the shining flesh
that will take over.

The step into
a wonderful vegetable
I hide,
and sleep,
and come out new
and blue
I step back,
one step,

but a million steps
to all
in the wooden world . . .
My old world . . .
my wooden world
seems old
seems dark
seems gruesome.
And all who live there,
without stepping
into the light
into the glow
are still speaking
the wooden language
that I have left behind
long ago.

                              Lyn Bigelow, 6th

Alone

I've travelled very far.
Where is my Ma?
I need her.
Do you need her?
I'm on a bird
who came from somewhere
and just appeared.
I need my Ma.
Where is she?
Is she very far?
I'm up real high
in the sky. But nowhere
can I find her.
I've been looking
for days and days
but where is she?
I need her.
I've been up in this
world for a month now
and I feel scared and left
out. Where am I?
I need my Ma.
Now I've been up here
for more than a year.
Where is my Ma?
I need her
I'm scared. Up on this
bird for more than a year
and a half now-but
where is my Ma? I'm still
scared-I still need her.
Here I am
still up in the air
But I didn't find my Ma
1 year 2 years 3 years now 4
I miss my Ma but am I here?
I've been alone on this bird
for four years.
I've been fine.
We were flying in a line
but my Ma never appeared.
Do I need my Ma?
I went this far without her
for four years.
I've been fine. I guess
I don't need her.
I haven't been with her.
Could I go on forever
like this?

But do I need my Ma?
Oh no I don't
I thought I did
but I don't
Now I'll live happily ever after.
                    Tina Pizzuti, 6th

Gifts

I give you a handful of marbles.
They are a cluster of fish eggs.
I give you life.

I give you a pair of marbles.
They are the moon looking
at its reflection in a lake.
I give you beauty.

I give you a marble.
It traps in itself
only a few things.
This makes me look closely
and realize that everything
is important.
I give you wisdom.

                    Gretchen Schuessler, 6th

My Kaleidoscope

My kaleidoscope holds the meaning of life
always changing its ways,
different colors and shapes. It holds
the fragments of my life. I love my
kaleidoscope, it changes every mood,
it's my moody scope, it's sad, it's forlorn,
it's angry, it's falling down through the stars,
it's a drowning rock thrown into the sea.
It's a raindrop falling into a well,
my feelings are different, they change,
I don't know my inner feelings any more,
my kaleidoscope holds my feelings
that I never told a soul,
the peace and shadows are the whispers of my
                    dreams.
This is my kaleidoscope.

                    Caitlin Pessin, 6th

The Violin Circle

On its side
the violin lies waiting,
waiting to come alive again.
Its youthful player
who wove a timeless symphony
is gone now.
His instrument has fallen silent,
gathering dust
in a distant room.
Generations later
two gnarled hands
pass it lovingly
to a grandchild.
The youthful player
holds it gently once again,
touching old grooves
with infinite care.
Drawing her bow across the strings,
the child resumes the ageless symphony,
knitting together past and present
in the harmony of sound.

Marya Cohen, 8th

The Four Seasons

Spring.
Spring is a robin with spring in its beak
It flies over the world and spring drops
from the robin's beak and spreads all over
the world.

Summer.
Summer is God's stove.
Right after spring comes
and ends, it is God's winter.
He keeps warm by turning on his stove.
The heat comes down to earth
and makes it hotter than spring.

Also, summer is a baseball player hitting
He hits the summer ball down to earth
It exploded all over earth bringing us warmth.
That's summer.

Fall.
Fall is the birds flying south.
They grab summer and take it home with them.
Right after they grab summer,
a new page is put on.
The summer page is ripped off
and the fall page is left.

Winter.
Winter is a polar bear with winter on its tail.
Winter is trying to pull the polar bear back,
but the polar bear pulls it all over the world.
Soon winter is gone, but we go back to spring.

T.R. Gilmore, 5th

How I Write Poems

I asked a group of students who had been drawing and writing poems, songs, and stories all year, how they felt when they were thinking and writing.

I think about it all the time. I lay in
bed just thinking for the words. The next day
I write up my ideas in my journal, the words
come right out of my brain. It feels like
I'm floating around in an ocean of words.

                    Benjamin Gaydos, 4th

First it starts from my fingers.
I feel and I touch. Then with my nose
I smell. Then with my ears I can hear.
My eyes. My whole body figures how to get
a poem. I like writing poems when I'm quiet.
You have to be honest with yourself.

                    Jeffrey Venter, 5th

(from an Interview with Tom Moscovitch in Kindergarten)

". . . when you're finished, it's not very exciting,
because you don't get to work on it . . . I don't
know what I'm going to draw, then I start
drawing. I still don't know what I'm going to
draw when I'm drawing it . . . . when I think of
one, the picture's all finished, that I wanted. I
don't even know I made it."

How I Write Poems

I walk by a dandelion blowing in the breeze,
That gives me an idea for a poem,
my mind fills up to the top
with ideas and the ideas
even go down to my knees,
soon they will be down
to my feet, and I will be
so full I will pop.
I run to find a paper,
I hop to find a paper,
I jump to find a paper,
I find a paper,
my mind is empty,
my knees are empty,
my feet are empty,
but my paper is full.

                    Abigail Drescher, 4th

Birth

The seed is planted
Nourished
Worried into fragments
Unified in a dream
Discharged from the earth
With a force unimaginable
Birthed into awakening.
Pleasure seeps through its veins
Joy lights up its face.
A poem is born.

                    Carol Bearse, 4/5 teacher

Stairways

Poems start as thought or emotions,
but not all turn into poems. They have to
choose the right doors and paths and go
through valleys and over mountains that
have glowing rivers of ideas.

Even if the right trails are taken,
there's still stairways to be climbed.
So the thoughts will climb the stairways
and reach a rainbow surrounded by pearl
white clouds.

                    Tom Fowler, 5th

Wings

Lorenzo
Wrote a poem
About a Hitchhawk
How that bird could fly
Fly high and mean and strong
Fly like smoke
Like a terrible kite
Fly out and into light
Out doors and windows long green corridors
Basement lavatory principal's office
Nurse's room Out the center
Of the desk The bird could wing it
Teacher say This the first thing
Lorenzo here has done all year
Most likely be the last
Lorenzo smile
A high dark smile
He knew the bird could fly
He knew how wicked well
He knew how shining
Lovely was the
Flight

Elizabeth McKim

Every Poem Is An Emergency

The child has finally written
the poem she cannot write.
She runs to the woman
whom she knows will know
what she has done but the
woman is somewhere else
and the child cannot just
leave the poem on the woman's
desk or simply wait until
tomorrow, the poem must be
given from the child's hot
hand into the woman's and
it must be now. The child
knows now that she can write
the poem and understands
that as suddenly as it comes
into her heart, it must be
shared. Inside her body,
there are sirens and flashing
lights, adrenalin courses,
her pulse accelerates.
This is a matter of life.
The poem, once written
must be given now.

Judith Steinbergh

A Poem Is My Gift to You

A poem is my gift to you
and your gift to me.
A poem is my treasure.
It carries me on magic wings
to great adventures.
A poem is my power.
It can disguise me
or reveal who I truly am.
I am a mountain,
standing tall, unmoving.
A poem is my creation.
I feed it, shelter it,
wrap it in silver paper.
A poem is my gift to you
and your gift to me.

Gretchen Schuessler, 6th

GoodBye

I'll miss you
I know you'll
be back but
I'm impatient
but don't think
poetry has left
my heart you
have put it there
it will stay there
forever and ever...

Ryan McCarthy, 2nd

RECOMMENDED READINGS AND RESOURCES FOR TEACHING POETRY: SELECTED BIBLIOGRAPHY

© 1999 by Judith Steinbergh and Elizabeth McKim

We have revised this bibliography for our third printing because there have been so many important and beautiful new poetry books. By the time Beyond Words goes to press, there will be even more insightful, engaging, accessible poetry books for students of all ages and from all cultures and backgrounds. We want teachers and students to use this bibliography and to know that we also have delighted in and learned from these books. Even those volumes which are out of print are worth tracking down in libraries. While we have listed the books under three age groups, these divisions are somewhat arbitrary. Many books contain poems that are appropriate for students of various ages and abilities. We have also included a separate section of poetry resources for teachers. We feel it is essential for librarians and teachers to familiarize themselves with a wide range of available books so they can better serve their young poets.

GRADES K-3

Ada, Alma Flor, *Gathering the Sun: An Alphabet in Spanish and English*, translated by Rosa Zubizarreta, illustrated by Simón Silva, Lothrop, Lee & Shepard, New York, 1997.

Adoff, Arnold, *Eats*, Lothrop, Lee & Shepard, New York, 1979.

Adoff, Arnold, *In for Winter, Out for Spring*, Harcourt Brace, New York, 1991.

Adoff, Arnold, ed., *My Black Me*, Dutton, New York, l974. A beginning book of black poetry.

Adoff, Arnold, *Sports Pages*, J. P. Lippincott, New York, 1986.

Asch, Frank, *Cactus Poems*, photographs by Ted Levin, A Gulliver Green Book/Harcourt Brace, New York, 1998.

Bryan, Ashley, *Sing to the Sun: Poems and Pictures*, HarperCollins, New York, 1992.

Bryan, Ashly, ed. and illust., *ABC of African American Poetry,* Atheneum Books for Young Readers, Simon & Schuster, New York, 1997. Segments of poems selected by the artist.

Atwood, Ann, *Haiku: The Moon of the Earth*, Scribners, New York, 1971.

Baylor, Byrd, *Everybody Needs Rock*, Macmillan, New York, l974.

Baylor, Byrd, Hawk, *I Am Your Brother,* Aladdin Books, Macmillan, New York, l976. Story poems about Southwest Native American children and their experiences.

Baylor, Byrd, *If You Are a Hunter of Fossils*, Macmillan, New York, 1980.

Baylor, Byrd, *I'm In Charge of Celebrations*, Macmillan, New York, 1986.

Baylor, Byrd, *The Way to Start a Day*, Aladdin Books, Macmillan, New York, 1986.

Baylor, Byrd, *This Desert Is Theirs*, Aladdin Books, Macmillan, New York, 1975.

Baylor, Byrd, *When the Clay Sings*, Macmillan, New York, 1972.

Belting, Natalia M., *Our Fathers Had Powerful Songs*, E. P. Dutton, New York, 1974.

Belting, Natalia M., *The Sun is a Golden Earring*, Holt, Rinehart, New York, 1962. Myth poems from around the world.

Carle, Eric, *Dragons, Dragons, and Other Creatures that Never Were*, poems compiled by Laura Whipple, Philomel Books, New York, 1991.

Chandra, Deborah, *Balloons and Other Poems*, Sunburst, Farrar Straus Giroux, New York, 1990.

Clifton, Lucille, *Some of the Days of Everett Anderson*, Henry Holt, New York, 1970.

DePaola, Tomie, *Book of Poems*, Putnam, New York, 1988.

Diaz, Josemilio Gonzalez, *La Nina y el Cucubano*, Instituto de Cultura Puertorriquena, San Juan de Puerto Rico, 1985.

EDAF, *Rodando, Rodando*, Ediciones-Distribuciones, S. A., 1981.

Esbensen, Barbara Juster, *Cold Stars and Fireflies*, Crowell, New York, 1982.

Farber, Norma, *How Does It Feel to Be Old*, E. P. Dutton, New York, 1979.

Farber, Norma and Myra Cohn Livingston, eds., *These Small Stones*, Harper & Row, New York, 1987.

Florian, Douglas, *Insectlopedia*, Harcourt Brace, New York, 1998. Poems and paintings about many common insects.

Foster, John, ed., *A Second Poetry Book*, Oxford University Press, 1980.

Foster, John, ed., *A Very First Poetry Book*, Oxford University Press, 1984.

Fox, Siv Cedering, *The Blue Horse and Other Night Poems*, Seabury Press, New York, 1979.

Frost, Robert, *A Swinger of Birches*, poems selected by Barbara Holdridge, Stemmer House, Owings Mills, MD, 1982.

Giovanni, Nikki, *Spin a Soft Black Song*, Hill & Wang, New York, 1971.

Giovanni, Nikki, *Vacation Time*, William & Morrow, New York, 1980.

Glaser, Isabel Joshlin, ed., *Dreams of Glory: Poems Starring Girls*, Atheneum, Boston, 1995.

Greenfield, Eloise, *Daydreamers*, Dial, New York, 1981.

Greenfield, Eloise, *Honey, I Love*, Harper & Row, New York, 1978.

Greenfield, Eloise, *Nathaniel Talking*, Black Butterfly Children's Books, New York, 1988.

Greenfield, Eloise, *Night on Neighborhood Street*, Dial Books for Young Readers, New York, 1991.

Greenfield, Eloise, *Under the Sunday Tree*, Harper & Row, New York, 1988.

Griego, Margot C., Bucks, Gilbert and Kimball, eds., *Tortillitas para Mama and Other Nursery Rhymes, Spanish and English*, Holt, New York, 1981.

Grimes, Nikki, *It's Raining Laughter*, photographs by Myles C. Pinkney, Dial Books for Young Readers, New York, 1997.

Hall, Donald, *Ox-Cart Man*, Penguin Books, New York, 1979.

Ho, Minfong, ed., *Maples in the Mist: Children's Poems from the Tang Dynasty*, illustrated by Jean and Mou-sien Tseng, Lothrop, Lee & Shephard, New York, 1996. Poems in Chinese characters with English translations.

Hoberman, Mary Ann, *Fathers, Mothers, Sisters, Brothers: A Collection of Family Poems*, Little Brown, Boston, 1991.

Hopkins, Lee Bennett, ed., *Good Books, Good Times!*, HarperCollins, New York, 1990.

Hopkins, Lee Bennett, ed., *Places to Visit, Places to See*, (Also: *Families, Families*, and *Me, Myself and I!*) Sadlier-Oxford, New York, 1998.

Hopkins, Lee Bennett, ed., *Surprises, An I Can Read Book*, Harper & Row, New York, 1984.

Hopkins, Lee Bennett, ed., *The Sea is Calling Me*, Harcourt Brace, New York, l986.

Hopkins, Lee Bennett, ed., *The Sky is Full of Song*, Harper & Row, New York, l983.

Hudson, Wade, ed., *Pass It On: African-American Poetry for Children*, illustrated by Floyd Cooper, Scholastic, New York, 1993.

Hughes, Langston, *The Sweet and Sour Animal Book: Illustrated by Students from the Harlem School of the Arts*, Oxford University Press, New York, 1994. In 27 short and wonderfully clever poems, Langston Hughes takes children through both the alphabet and the animal world.

Janeczko, Paul B., ed., *Poetry from A to Z: A Guide for Young Writers*, Bradbury Press, New York, 1994.

Joseph, Lynn, *Coconut Kind of Day*: Island Poems, Lothrop, Lee & Shepard, New York, 1990.

Kolebka, Georges, *Petits Poèmes Pour Petites Mains*, Hatier, Paris, 1985.

Kuskin, Karla, *Any Me I Want to Be*, Harper & Row, New York, 1972. Includes animal and habitat riddle poems for young children.

Kuskin, Karla, *Near the Window Tree: Poems and Notes*, Harper & Row, New York, 1975.

Langstaff, John and Carol, *Shimmy Shimmy Coke-Ca-Pop*, Doubleday, Garden City, NJ, 1973.

Lenski, Lois, *City Poems*, Henry Z. Walck, Inc. New York, 1971.

Lewis, John, *The Chinese Word for Horse and Other Stories*, Schocken Books, New York, 1980.

Lewis, Richard, ed., *Miracles: Poems by English Speaking Children*, A Fireside Book/Simon & Schuster, New York, 1966.

Livingston, Myra Cohn, *Celebrations*, Holiday House, New York, 1985.

Livingston, Myra Cohn, ed., *I Like You If You Like Me*, Macmillan, New York, 1987.

Livingston, Myra Cohn, *Monkey Puzzle and Other Poems*, Atheneum, New York, 1984.

Livingston, Myra Cohn, ed., *Poems for Brothers, Poems for Sisters*, Holiday House, New York, 1991.

Livingston, Myra Cohn, ed., *Poems for Dogs*, Holiday House, New York, 1990.

Livingston, Myra Cohn, ed., *Poems for Fathers*, Holiday House, New York, 1989.

Livingston, Myra Cohn, ed., *Poems for Grandmothers*, Holiday House, New York, 1990.

Livingston, Myra Cohn, ed., *Poems for Mothers*, Holiday House, New York, 1988.

Livingston, Myra Cohn, ed., *Thanksgiving Poems*, Holiday House, New York, 1985.

McCord, David, *All Small*, Little Brown, Boston, 1986.

McCord, David, *The Star in the Pail*, Little Brown, Boston, 1925.

Martin, Bill, Jr. and John Archambault, *Knots on a Counting Rope*, Henry Holt, New York, 1966, 1987.

Moore, Lilian, *Think of Shadows*, Atheneum, New York, 1980.

Navasky, Bruno, ed. and trans., *Festival in My Heart: Poems by Japanese Children*, Harry N. Abrams, New York, 1993.

O'Neill, Mary, *Hailstones and Halibut Bones*, Doubleday, New York, 1961.

Pomerantz, Charlotte, *If I Had a Paka: Poems in Eleven Languages,* Green Willow Press, New York, 1982.

Prelutsky, Jack, *Something BIG Has Been Here*, Greenwillow Books, New York, 1990.

Prelutsky, Jack, ed., *The Beauty of the Beast: Poems from the Animal Kingdom*, Alfred A. Knopf, New York, 1997.

Rosen, Michael, J., ed., *Home*, A Charlotte Zolotow Book, HarperCollins, New York, 1992. A collaboration of thirty authors and illustrators to aid the homeless.

Sandburg, Carl, *Rainbows Are Made*, selected by Lee Bennett Hopkins, Hartcourt Brace, New York, 1982. Selections from Sandburg's work, suitable for young and middle grade children.

Shaw, Alison, ed. and photographer, *Until I Saw the Sea: A Collection of Seashore Poems*, Henry Holt, New York, 1995.

Silverstein, Shel, *Falling Up: Poems and Drawings,* HarperCollins, New York, 1996.

Silverstein, Shel, *The Light in the Attic,* Harper & Row, New York, 1981.

Silverstein, Shel, *Where the Sidewalk Ends*, Harper & Row, New York, 1974.

Singer, Marilyn, *Turtle in July*, Macmillan, New York, 1989.

Slier, Deborah, *Make a Joyful Sound: Poems for Children by African-American Poets*, Checkerboard Press, New York, 1991.

Sneve, Virginia, Driving Hawk*, Dancing Teepees*, Holiday House, New York, 1989.

Steinbergh, Judith and Cary Wolinsky, *Marshmallow Worlds*, Grosset & Dunlap, 1972. Poems and photos for children.

Steptoe, Javaka, ed. and illust., *In Daddy's Arms I Am Tall: African Americans Celebrating Fathers*, Lee & Low Books, New York, 1997.

Thomas, Joyce Carol, *Brown Honey in Broomwheat Tea*, illustrated by Floyd Cooper, HarperCollins, New York, 1993.

Torres, Pat, Jalygurr*: Aussie Animal Rhymes*, adapted from Kimberly Aboriginal Folk Stories, Yawuru Text by Jack Edgar, Elsie Edgar, and Thelma Saddler, Magabala Books, P. O. Box 668, Broome, West Australia, 1987.

Viorst, Judith, *If I Were in Charge of the World*, Aladdin, Macmillan, New York, 1981.

Walt Whitman, poems selected by Lee Bennett Hopkins, Harcourt Brace, New York, 1988.

Worth, Valerie, *All the Small Poems,* Sunburst Book/Farrar Straus Giroux, New York, 1987.

Yarbrough, Camille, *Cornrows*, Coward-McCann, New York, 1979.

Yolen, Jane, *Water Music: Poems for Children*, photographs by Jason Stemple, Wordsong/Boyds Mills Press, Honesdale, PA, 1995.

Zolotow, Charlotte, *Everything Glistens and Everything Sings*, Harcourt Brace Jovanovich, New York, 1987.

GRADES 4-6 (many of the books for grades K-3 are still appropriate)

Adoff, Arnold, ed., *Celebrations: A New Anthology of Black American Poetry*, Follett, Chicago, 1977.

Adoff, ed., *I Am the Darker Brother*, Collier/Macmillan, New York, 1968.

Angelou, Maya, *Life Doesn't Frighten Me: Poems with Paintings by Jean-Michel Basquiat*, Stewart, Tabori & Chang, New York, 1993.

Arkhurst, Joyce C., compiling editor, *Have You Seen a Comet?: Children's Art and Writing from Around the World*, The John Day Co. in cooperation with the U. S. Committee for UNICEF, New York, 1971.

Bierhorst, John, ed., *In the Trail of the Wind*, Dell, New York, 1971. Native American poems.

California Poets in the Schools, *Forgotten Languages*, San Francisco, 1985. Multicultural anthology by California students and essay writers.

Cowing, Sue, ed., *Fire in the Sea: An Anthology of Poetry and Art*, A Kolowalu Book/University of Hawaii Press, The Honolulu Academey of the Arts, Honolulu, 1966.

Cumpián, Carlos, *Latino Rainbow: Poems about Latino Americans*, illustrated by Richard Leonard, Childrens Press, Chicago, 1994.

Dickinson, Emily, *A Brighter Garden*, poetry collected by Karen Ackerman, Philomel Books/ The Putnam & Grosset Group, New York, 1990.

Downie, Mary Alice and Barbara Robertson, eds., *The New Wind Has Wings: Poems from Canada*, Oxford University Press, 1984.

Dunning, Stephen, Edward Lueders and Hugh Smith, eds., *Reflections on a Gift of Watermelon Pickle*, Lothrop, Lee & Shephard Co., New York, 1967.

Dunning, Stephen, Edward Lueders and Hugh Smith, eds., *Some Haystacks Don't Even Have Any Needles*, Lothrop, Lee & Shephard Co., New York, 1969.

Farrell, Kate, ed., *Art & Nature: An Illustrated Anthology of Nature Poetry*, A Bulfinch Press Book/Little Brown, Boston, 1992. Art from the Metropolitan Museum of Art, New York.

Feelings, Tom, ed. and illust., *Soul Looks Back in Wonder*, Dial Books, New York, 1993.

Fields, Julia, *The Green Lion of Zion Street*, Margaret K. McElderry Books, New York, 1988.

Fleischman, Paul, *I Am Phoenix: Poems for Two Voices*, Harper & Row, New York, 1985.

Fleischman, Paul, *Joyful Noise: Poems for Two Voices*, Harper & Row, New York, 1988.

Foster, John, ed., *Let's Celebrate: Festival Poems*, Oxford University Press, 1989.

Faulkner, Karin and Daryl Chinn, eds., *A Chant a Mile Long*, California Poets in the Schools, Student Anthology, San Francisco, 1990.

Harjo, Joy, and Stephen Strom, *Secrets from the Center of the World*, Sun Tracks and the University of Arizona Press, Tucson, 1989.

Hughes, Ted, *Season Song*, Viking, New York, 1975.

Janeczko, Paul B., ed., *Going Over to Your Place: Poems for Each Other*, Bradbury Press, New York, 1987.

Janeczko, Paul B., ed., *Pocket Poems*, Bradbury Press, New York, 1985.

Janeczko, Paul B., ed., *Strings: A Gathering of Family Poems*, Bradbury Press, Scarsdale, NY, 1984.

Janeczko, Paul B., ed., *The Music of What Happens: Poems that Tell Stories*, Orchard Books, New York, 1988.

Janeczko, Paul B., ed., *The Place My Words Are Looking For*, Bradbury Press, New York, 1990.

Janeczko, Paul B., *The Sweet Diamond: Baseball Poems*, illustrated by Carole Katchen, Atheneum Books for Young Readers/Simon & Schuster, New York, 1998.

Janeczko, Paul B., ed., *This Delicious Day*, Orchard Books, New York, 1987.

Jeffers, Susan, illust., *Brother Eagle, Sister Sky*, Dial Books, New York, 1991. Paintings to text spoken by Chief Seattle.

Kennedy, X. J., *Did Adam Name the Vinegarroon?*, David Godine, Boston, 1982.

Koch, Kenneth and Kate Farrell, *Talking to the Sun*, Metropolitan Museum of Art/Holt Rinehart, New York, 1985.

Kumin, Maxine, *The Microscope*, Harper & Row, New York, 1968.

Larrick, Nancy, ed., *Bring Me All of Your Dreams*, M. Evans, New York, 1980.

Larrick, Nancy, ed., *Crazy to Be Alive in Such a Strange World*, M. Evans, New York, 1977.

Larrick, Nancy, ed., *On City Streets*, M. Evans, New York, 1968.

Larrick, Nancy, ed., *Room for Me and a Mountain Lion*, M. Evans, New York, 1974.

Lawrence, D. H., *Birds, Beasts and the Third Thing*, Viking, New York, 1964.

Lessac, Frané, *Caribbean Canvas: Paintings of the Islands with Poetry by Caribbean Poets*, J. B. Lippincott, New York, 1987.

Lewis, J. Patrick, *Black Swan White Crow*, Atheneum, New York, 1995. A fine collection of Haiku and woodcuts appropriate for any age.

Lewis, Richard, ed., *Miracles: Poems by Children*, Simon & Schuster, New York, 1966.

Lewis, Richard, ed., *Out of the Earth I Sing: Poetry and Songs of Primitive Peoples of the World*, Norton, New York, 1968.

Lewis, Richard, ed., *Still Waters of the Air: Poems by Three Modern Spanish Poets*, The Dial Press, New York, 1970.

Lewis, Richard, ed., *The Luminous Landscape: Chinese Art and Poetry*, Doubleday, Garden City, NJ.

Livingston, Myra Cohn, *Earth Songs*, Holiday House, New York, 1986.

Livingston, Myra Cohn, *Sea Songs*, Holiday House, New York, 1986.

Livingston, Myra Cohn, *Sky Songs*, Holiday House, New York, 1984.

Livingston, Myra Cohn, *Space Songs*, Holiday House, New York, 1988.

Morrison, Lillian, ed., *Rhythm Road: Poems To Move To*, Lothrop Lee, New York, 1988.

Morrison, Lillian, ed., *Slam Dunk: Basketball Poems,* Hyperion Books for Children, New York, 1995.

Myers, Walter Dean, *Harlem: A Poem with Pictures by Christopher Myers*, Scholastic, New York, 1997.

Nichols, Judith, ed., *What on Earth...?: Poems with a Conservation Theme*, Faber & Faber, London, 1989.

Orska, Krystyna, Illustrated Poems, Hubbard Press, Northbrook, IL, 1973.

Shahib Nye, Naomi, ed., *The Space Between Our Footsteps: Poems and Paintings from the Middle East*, Simon & Schuster Books for Young Readers, New York, 1998.

Simon, Seymour, ed., *Star Walk*, Morrow Junior Books, New York, 1995. A collection of poems and
photographs about stars and space.

Steele, Susanna and Morag Styles, *Mother Gave a Shout, Poems by Women and Girls*,
Volcano Press, P. O. Box 270, Volcano, CA 95689, 1991.

Strickland, Dorothy, ed., *Listen Children: An Anthology of Black Literature*, Bantam, New York, 1982.

Sullivan, Charles, ed., *Children of Promise: African-American Literature and Art for Young People*,
Harry N. Abrams, New York, 1991.

Sullivan, Charles, ed., *Imaginary Animals: Poetry and Art for Young People*, Harry N. Abrams, New York, 1996.

Weiss, Renee Karol, *A Paper Zoo: A Collection of Animal Poems by Modern American Poets*, Macmillan, New York, 1968.

Yan, Ke, *Poems on a Boy's Paintings*, Foreign Language Press, Beijing, China, 1981. Color paintings by a young
Chinese boy with poems in Chinese by a Chinese poet with English translations.

Yolen, Jane, *Bird Watch*, Philomel Books/The Putnam & Grosset Group, New York, 1990.

Yolen, Jane, ed., *Mother Earth, Father Sky: Poems of Our Planet*, illustrated by Jennifer Hewitson,
Wordsong/Boyds Mills Press, Honesdale, PA, 1996.

Yolen, Jane, *Ring of Earth: A Child's Book of Seasons*, illustrated by John Wallner, Harcourt Brace Jovanovich,
New York, 1986.

Young, Ed, *Voices of the Heart*, Scholastic Press, New York, 1997. Collage illustrations of Chinese characters
and the artist's lyrical explorations of the emotions the images convey.

GRADES 7, 8 and up (Many of the 4-6 books are still appropriate here.)

Adoff, Arnold, *Poetry of Black America*, Harper & Row, New York, 1973.

Awiakta, Marilou, *Abiding Appalachia*, St. Lukes Press, Memphis, TN, 1978. Native American poet.

Ayumi: A Japanese American Anthology, P. O. Box 5024, San Francisco, CA 94101, 1980.

Becker, Robin, *All American Girl*, University of Pittsburgh Press, 1996. One woman's journey of
finding sexual, gender, and artistic identity. Engaging humor and integrity. Best for high school students.

Berry, James, *When I Dance*, Harcourt Brace Jovanovich, New York, 1991, 1988. Poems which draw
their inspiration from inner-city life of Britain and from the rural Caribbean.

Brathwaite, Edward Kamau, *Mother Poems*, Oxford University Press, 1977. Caribbean poet.

Bruchac, Joseph, ed., *Breaking Silence: An Anthology of Contemporary Asian American Poets*,
Greenfield Review Press, Greenfield Center, NY, 1983.

Bruchac, Joseph, ed., *Songs from this Earth on Turtle's Back*, Greenfield Review Press, Greenfield Center, NY, 1983.

Buchwalk, Emilie and Ruth Roston, eds., *This Sporting Life*, Milkweed Editions, Minneapolis, 1987.

Carlson, Lori M., ed., *Cool Salsa: Bilingual Poems on Growing Up Latino in the US*, Fawcett Juniper, New York, 1994.

Chin, Marilyn, *Dwarf Bamboo*, Greenfield Review Press, Greenfield Center, NY, 1987.

Chinn, Daryl Ngee, *Soft Parts of the Back*, University of Central Florida Press, Orlando, 1989.

Cornish, Sam, 1935, *A Memoir*, Ploughshares, Boston, 1990. Powerful poetic memoir of growing
up Black in Baltimore during the Depression and World War II.

Ellman, Richard, and Robert O'Clair, *The Norton Anthology of Modern Poetry*, W. W. Norton, New York, 1973.

Empringham, Toni, ed., *Fiesta in Aztlan: Chicano Poetry*, Capra Press, Santa Barbara, 1982.

Ferlinghetti, Lawrence, *Pictures of the Gone World*, Pocket Poets, San Francisco, 1955.

Ford, R. A. D., trans., *Russian Poetry: A Personal Anthology*, Mosiac Press, Canada, 1984.

Foss, Phillip, ed., *The Clouds Threw This Light*, Institute of American Indian Arts Press, Santa Fe, NM, 1983.

Harris, Marie and Kathleen Aguero, *An Ear to the Ground*, University of Georgia Press, Athens, 1989.

Harrison, Michael, and Christopher Stuart-Clark, eds., *Peace and War*, Oxford University Press, New York, 1989.

Heany, Seamus and Ted Hughes, eds., *The Rattle Bag*, Faber & Faber, London, 1982.

Herrera, Juan Felipe, *Laughing Out Loud I Fly: Poems In English and Spanish*, Joanna Cotler Books, New York, 1998.
A whimsical and engaging collection of poems by one of the leading Chicano poets.

Hesse, Karen, *Out of the Dust: A Novel*, Scholastic, New York, 1997. A novel in poetry.

Hirshfield, Jane, ed., *Women In Praise of The Sacred: 43 Centuries of Spiritual Poetry by Women*,
Harper Perennial, New York, 1994.

Howe, Florence and Ellen Bass, eds., *No More Masks!: An Anthology of Poems by Women*, Anchor/Doubleday, New York, 1973.

Janeczko, Paul B., *Poetspeak: In their Work and about their Work*, Bradbury Press, Scarsdale, NY, 1983.

Jordan, June, ed., *Soulscript: Afro-American Poetry*, Zenith/Doubleday, New York, 1970.
The first section has poems by Black teenagers, many of whom are grown and successful poets now.

Kherdian, David, ed., *I Sing the Song of Myself*, Greenwillow, New York, 1978. An anthology of autobiographical poetry appropriate for sixth grade and up.

Knudson, R. R. and May Swenson, eds., *American Sports Poems*, Orchard Books, New York, 1988.

Komunyakaa, Yusef, *Dien Cai Dau*, Wesleyan University Press, Middletown, CT, 1988. Poems about Vietnam. Best for high school students.

Lee, Li-Young , *The Winged Seed: A Remembrance*, Simon & Schuster, New York, 1995. An intense and poetic memoir that follows the journey that began in the 1950s when Lee's family fled from China.

Lorie, Dick and Mark Pawlak, eds., *Smart Like Me: High School Age Writing*, Hanging Loose Press, Brooklyn, NY, 1989.

Lowenfels, Walter, *The Writing on the Wall*, Doubleday, New York, 1969. Poems about social and political issues.

Lueders, Edward and Primus St. John, *Zero Makes Me Happy*, Scott, Foresman, Glenview, IL, 1976.

Mazer, Norma Fox and Marjorie Lewis, eds., *Waltzing on Water: Poetry by Women*, Dell, 1989.

Merriam, Eve, *If Only I Could Tell You*, Knopf, New York, 1983. Poems about love.

Miller, E. Ethelbert, ed., *In Search of Color Everywhere: A Collection of African-American Poetry*, Stewart, Tabori & Chang, New York, 1994.

Milosz, Czeslaw, ed., *A Book of Luminous Things: An International Anthology of Poetry*, Harcourt Brace & Company, New York, 1996. An accessible and illuminating anthology with annotations about each poem by Milosz.

Niatum, Duane, ed., *Harper's Anthology of Twentieth Century Native American Poetry*, Harper & Row, New York, 1988.

Oresick, Peter and Nicholas Coles, *Working Classics: Poems on Industrial Life*, University of Illinois Press, Urbana, 1990.

Peck, Richard, ed., *Mindscapes: Poems for the Real World*, Laurel-Leaf Contemporary Literature/Dell, New York, 1971 and 1990.

Peck, Richard, ed., *Sounds and Silences: Poetry for Now*, Delecorte, New York, 1970.

Piercy, Marge, ed., *Early Ripening: American Women's Poetry Now*, Pandora Press, London. 1988.

Piercy, Marge, *Eight Chambers of the Heart: Selected Poems*, Penguin, London, 1995.

Reed, John and Clive Wake, *A New Book of African Verse*, Heinemann Ltd., London, 1984.

Ritchie, Elisavietta, ed., *The Dolphin's Arc*, SCOP Publications, College Park, MD, 1989.

Rosenberg, Liz, ed., *Earth-Shattering Poems*, Henry Holt, New York, 1998. A small collection of intense poems from Sappho to the present.

Rosenberg, Liz, ed., *The Invisible Ladder: An Anthology of Contemporary American Poems for Young Readers*, Henry Holt, New York, 1996. Includes brief comments by the poets.

Rothenberg, Jerome, ed., *Shaking the Pumpkin: Traditional Poetry of the Indian North Americas*, Doubleday, New York, 1972.

Rothenberg, Jerome, ed., *Technicians of the Sacred*, Anchor/Doubleday, New York, 1968. A range of poetries from Africa, America, Asia, and Oceana. This anthology of poetry and chant from tribal cultures around the world illuminates the oral tradition of poetry and reveals many techniques which modern-day poets have incorporated into their own writing.

Rubin, Robert Alden, ed., *Poetry Out Loud*, Algonquin Books/Chapel Hill/Workman, New York, 1993.
Over 100 great poems to dramatize or perform.

Rylant, Cynthia, Soda Jerk, *Beech Tree Books*, William & Morrow, New York, 1990.

Rylant, Cynthia, *Something Permanent*, Harcourt Brace, New York, 1994. A hauntingly beautiful collection of Walker Evans photos and poems of place and persona.

Salkey, Andrew, ed., *Breaklight: the Poetry of the Caribbean*, Doubleday, New York, 1972.

Shange, Ntozake, *I live in music*, paintings by Romaire Bearden, Stewart, Tabori, & Chang, New York, 1994.
Visually dazzling and verbally dancing book.

Shihab Nye, Naomi, and Paul B. Janeczko, eds., *I Feel a Little Jumpy Around You: A Book of Her Poems and His Poems Collected in Pairs*, Simon & Schuster Books for Young Readers, 1996.

Shihab Nye, Naomi, ed., *This Same Sky: A Collection of Poems from around the World*, Four Winds Press, New York, 1992. A substantial collection representing the world's cultures, in English translation.

Soto, Gary, *A Fire in My Hands: A Book of Poems*, Scholastic, New York, 1990.

Soto, Gary, *Neighborhood Odes*, Scholastic, New York, 1994.

Soto, Gary, *New and Selected Poems*, Chronicle, San Francisco, 1995.

Stetson, Erlene, ed., *Black Sister: Poetry by Black American Women, 1746-1980*, Indiana University Press, Bloomington, 1981.

Strickland, Dorothy, ed., *Listen Children: An Anthology of Black Literature*, Bantam, New York, 1982.

Sullivan, Charles, ed., *Here Is My Kingdom: Hispanic-American Literature and Art for Young People*, Harry N. Abrams, New York, 1994.

Sylvain, Patrick, *Butterfly Wings (Zel Papiyon): A Collection of Poems for Young Adults in English and Haitian Creole*, 14 Hamilton Road, Somerville, MA 02144, 1994.

Thompson, Eileen, *Experiencing Poetry*, Globe Books, New York, 1987. Excellent selection of poems, response questions, and writing suggestions for middle grade students 5-9.

Weaver, Michael S., *Timber and Prayer: The Indian Pond Poems*, University of Pittsburgh Press, Pittsburgh, 1996.

Willard, Nancy, ed., *Step Lightly: Poems for the Journey*, Harcourt Brace, New York, 1998. An accessible and strong anthology.

FOR TEACHERS

Atwell, Nancie, *In the Middle: New Understandings about Writing, Reading, and Learning, 2nd ed.*, Boynton/Cook, Portsmouth, NH, 1998.

Behn, Robin and Chase Twichell, eds., *The Practice of Poetry: Writing Exercises from Poets Who Teach*, HarperPerennial/HarperCollins, New York, 1992. Poetry writing exercises for adults and older students.

Brown, Bill and Malcolm Glass, *Important Words: A Book for Poets and Writers*, Boynton/Cook/Heinemann, Portsmouth, NH, 1991.

Bunchman, Janis and Stephanie Bissell Briggs, *Pictures & Poetry*, Davis Publications, Worcester, MA, 1994. Inspiring lessons on creating poetry and art. In color.

California Poets in the Schools, *The Boy Who Heard a Voice: 25th Anniversary Issue,* California Poets in the Schools, 2845 24th Street, San Francisco, CA 94110, 1989. Poems and essays by students, teachers, and poet-teachers. CPITS publishes a catalogue of anthologies and resources for teaching of writing.

Center for the Arts of Indian America, *Art and Indian Children*, Curriculum Bulletin No. 7, Box 40591, Palisades Station, Washington, DC 20016, reprinted March 1975.

Center for the Arts of Indian America, *My Music Reaches to the Sky*, Box 40591, Palisades Station, Washington, DC 20016, 1973.

Chatton, Barbara, *Using Poetry across the Curriculum: A Whole Language Approach,* The Oryx Press, 4041 North Central at Indian School Road, Phoenix, AZ 85012, 1993.

Chatwin, Bruce, *Songlines*, Penguin Books, New York, 1987.

Denman, Gregory A., *When You've Made It Your Own: Teaching Poetry to Young People*, Heinemann, Portsmouth, NH, 1988.

Deutsch, Babette, *Poetry Handbook: A Dictionary of Terms, 4th ed.*, Perennial Library/Harper & Row, New York, 1957, 1974.

Dillard, Annie, *Pilgrim at Tinker Creek*, Harper's Magazine Press, New York, 1974. Although not directly about teaching poetry, this book written by a naturalist and poet, helps us intensify our ability to see and experience the world around us.

Esbensen, Barbara Juster, *A Celebration of Bees: Helping Children to Write Poetry*, Henry Holt, New York, 1975, 1995.

Fox, John, *Finding What You Didn't Lose: Expressing Your Truth and Creativity through Poem Making*, Tarcher/Putnam, New York, 1995.

Fox, John, *Poetic Medicine: The Healing Art of Poem-Making*, Tarcher/Putnam, New York, 1998.

150

Gensler, Kinereth and Nina Nyhart, *The Poetry Connection, Teachers and Writers Collaborative,*
5 Union Square West, New York, NY 10003, 1978. This book offers many suggestions for poetry writing
sessions along with an excellent compilation of examples by adult poets and children.

Goldberg, Natalie, *Wild Mind*, Bantam, New York, 1990. Wonderful exercises to motivate the adult and adolescent
writer to practice writing.

Goldberg, Natalie, *Writing Down the Bones*, Shambala Press, New York, 1986.

Goss, Linda and Marian E. Barnes, *Talk that Talk: Afro-American Oral Tradition,*
Touchstone/Simon & Schuster, New York, 1989.

Griffin, Shaun, ed., *Desert Wood: An Anthology of Nevada Poets*, University of Nevada Press, Reno, 1991.

Grossman, Florence, *Listening to the Bells: Learning to Read Poetry by Writing Poetry*, Boynton/Cook/Heinemann,
Portsmouth, NH, 1991.

Heard, Georgie, *For the Good of the Earth and the Sun*, Heinemann, Portsmouth, NH, 1989.

Hernandez Cruz, Victor, *Red Beans*, Coffee House Press, Minneapolis, 1991. Essays and poetry by a Chicano writer.

Hoffman, Eva, *Lost in Translation: A Life in a New Language*, E. P. Dutton, New York, 1989.

Hopkins, Lee Bennett, *Pass the Poetry, Please!*, Harper & Row, New York, 1972.

Hughes, Ted, *Poetry in the Making*, Faber & Faber, Boston, 1967.
A lively discussion of the process of writing poetry with several thematic areas described in depth.

Jackson, Jacqueline, *Turn Not Pale Beloved Snail*, Little Brown, Boston, 1974. Written by the author of many children's
books, this book is filled with ideas for observing the world around us with all of our senses. Written in a
conversational tone with examples from children's literature, this book appeals to adults and to children in
fifth grade and up.

Janeczko, Paul B., *Favorite Poetry Lessons: Grades 4-8*, Scholastic, New York, 1998.

Johnson, David, M., *Word Weaving: A Creative Approach to Teaching and Writing Poetry*, NCTE, Urbana, IL, 1990.

Kennedy, X. J. and Dorothy, *Knock at a Star: A Child's Introduction to Poetry*. Little Brown, Boston, 1982.

Koch, Kenneth, Rose, *Where Did You Get that Red?*, Random House, New York, 1973. Koch suggests ways to use
"classic" poems as models for teaching poetry to children. Specific poems are included in the book.

Koch, Kenneth, *Wishes, Lies, and Dreams: Teaching Children to Write Poetry*, Chelsea House, New York, 1970.
Koch documents his work as one of the first Poets-in-the Schools. Using examples from children in the
New York Public Schools, he lays out simple exercises for children.

Kowit, Steve, *In the Palm of Your Hand: The Poet's Portable Workshop*, Tilbury House, Gardiner, ME, 1995.

Larrick, Nancy, ed., *Somebody Turned a Tap On in These Kids*, Delacorte Press, New York, 1971. A collection of
talks on teaching poetry to children.

Levine, Steven K. and Ellen G., *Foundations of Expressive Arts Therapy: Theoretical and Clinical Perspectives,*
Jessica Kingsley, London, 1998. McKim has a chapter entitled "Poetry: Serious Play with Words," which
gives a focused perspective on her poetry work with children, teachers, and expressive arts therapists.

Lewis, Claudia, *A Big Bite of the World*, Prentice-Hall, New York, 1979. Ideas for and examples of children's creative
writing by age group. She discusses ways to integrate creative writing into the classroom curriculum. This is
a lively and important work on writing with children by an experienced teacher and writer.

Lewis, Richard, Fire, *Fire Burning Bright: Six Radio Programs on the Nature and Origin of Poetry,*
The Touchstone Center, 141 East 88th Sreet, New York, NY 10028, 1985.

Livingston, Myra Cohn, *Poem-making: Ways to Begin Writing Poetry*, HarperCollins, New York, 1991.

Livingston, Myra Cohn, *The Child as Poet: Myth or Reality*, Horn, Boston, 1984.

Lopate, Philip, *Being with Children*, Bantam, New York, 1975. A personal account of a poet's experience working
in one urban school in the fields of poetry, theatre, radio, and video.

Lopate, Philip, ed., *Journal of a Living Experiment, Teachers and Writers*, New York, 1985. A History of Teachers
and Writers Collaborative.

Lown, Fredric, *Langston Hughes: An Interdisciplinary Biography*, J. Weston Walch, Portland, ME, 1997.

Lown, Fredric and Judith Steinbergh, *Reading and Writing Poetry with Teenagers*, J. Weston Walch,
Portland, ME, 1996. Extensive poetry units for grades 7-12.

Marzán, Julio, ed., *Luna, Luna: Creative Writing Ideas from Spanish, Latin American, and Latino Literature*, Teachers
and Writers Collaborative, New York, 1997.

Nims, John Frederick, *Western Wind*, Random House, New York, 1974. This is an excellent high school and college level text.

Oliver, Mary, *A Poetry Handbook*, A Harvest Original/Harcourt Brace, New York, 1994. A lyrical, inspiring guide for beginning writers.

Oliver, Mary, *Rules of the Dance: A Handbook for Writing and Reading Metrical Verse*, A Mariner Original/Houghton Mifflin, Boston, 1998.

Pack, Robert and Jay Parini, eds., *Introspections: American Poets on One of Their Own Poems*, Middlebury College Press, Hanover, NH, 1997. These insightful essays about poems are geared to older students.

Padgett, Ron, ed., *Handbook of Poetic Forms, Teachers and Writers Collaborative*, New York, 1988.

Phillips, Rodney, *The Hand of the Poet: Poems and Papers in Manuscript*, Rizzoli, New York, 1997. Short biographies, poems, original manuscript and revision markings of 100 poets.

Piercy, Marge, *Parti-Colored Blocks for a Quilt*, Univeristy of Michigan Press, Ann Arbor, 1982. Essays and interviews with this powerful and prolific poet and novelist. This is part of an excellent series published by University of Michigan Press titled: Writers on Writing.

Richards, M. C., *Centering*, Wesleyan University Press, Middletown, CN, 1962. Reflections on the similarities and differences in the process of making pottery and poetry.

Rigg, Pat and Virginia G. Allen, *When They Don't All Speak English: Integrating the ESL student into the Regular Classroom*, NCTE, Urbana, IL, 1989.

Richardson, Elwyn, *In the Early World*, Pantheon, New York, 1964.

Robinson, Sandy, *Origins,* Teachers and Writers, New York, 1989. How to investigate word roots with children.

Simonson, Rick and Scott Walker, *Multi-Cultural Literacy*, Graywolf, St. Paul, MN, 1988.

Stafford, William, *Writing the Australian Crawl*, University of Michigan Press, Ann Arbor, 1978. A readable, illuminating, and inspiring collection of essays, interviews, and conversations by the well known poet, William Stafford, focusing on his process and philosophy of writing.

Steinbergh, Judith, *Reading and Writing Poetry, Grades K-4*, Scholastic, New York, 1994.

Steinbergh, Judith, "To Arrive in Another World: Poetry, Language Development, and Culture," in *Arts As Education*, edited by Merryl Goldberg and Ann Phillips, Reprint Series No. 24, Harvard Educational Review, 6 Appian Way, Cambridge, MA 02138, 1992.

Steinbergh, Judith and Victor Cockburn, *Where I Come From!: Songs and Poems from Many Cultures*, Talking Stone Press, 99 Evans Road, Brookline, MA 02445, 1991. Sixty-three poems and songs in 12 languages with translations from the USA and around the world. Two tape cassettes and a booklet.

Thomas, Lorenzo, ed., *Sing the Sun Up: Creative Writing Ideas from African American Literature*, Teachers and Writers Collaborative, New York, 1998.

Tsujimoto, Joseph I., *Teaching Poetry Writing to Adolescents*, NCTE, Urbana, IL 1964.

Walker, Margaret, *How I Wrote Jubilee and Other Essays on Life and Literature*, The Feminist Press, New York, 1990.

Watershed Foundation's Poets' Audio Center, *Poetry on Tape Catalog*, P. O. Box 50145, Washington, DC 20091.

Whitman, Ruth and Harriet Feinberg, eds., *Poemmaking*, Mass. Council of Teachers of English, Boston, 1975. A collection of essays by Massachusetts Poets in the Schools.

Wooldridge, Susan G., *Poemcrazy: freeing your life with words*, Three Rivers Press, New York, 1996. Reflections and exercises on writing poetry.

Zavatsky, Bill and Ron Padgett, eds., *The Whole Word Catalogues I and II*, McGraw-Hill Paperbacks in association with Teachers and Writers Collaborative, New York, 1977. An extensive and varied collection of ideas by teachers and writers for teaching writing to children.

A LETTER TO OUR READERS

Judith and I are delighted that our book has gone into its third printing. To be honest, we had no idea in the beginning how far *Beyond Words* would travel! Since the early eighties, we have had the opportunity to help teachers learn more about poetry ideas and inspirations for writing, sharing of poems, ways to weave them into curricula and connect them to the other arts. In this endeavor, I have traveled to many places throughout the United States and abroad: from Milwaukee to El Paso, from Toronto to Tel Aviv. Everywhere I go, teachers have told me what an essential and resourceful guide this book has been to them. I am glad because Judith and I made this book with teachers respectfully in mind. I feel in many ways that it's a book made by all of us: teachers, poets, and students, and everywhere the many voices shine through in a rich tapestry of experience and culture.

Neither Judith nor I started out as artists sequestered in an ivory tower. We were journeywomen poets working in the community, traveling up and around the poetry path, and we continue in this direction today, still spending time listening to the words of children. I often am humbled by the power of children's poetry, how well versed these young writers are at listening to the voices at work in the world around them, how closely they come to the heart of the matter, how adept they are at taking the big leaps, and how playful and purposeful they can be in their writing. I have been engaged with children and their words since the early seventies when I was poet-in-residence in the city of Brockton and a small boy listened to the haunting sounds of the humpback whale. Because he had minimal writing skills, he picked up my tape recorder and whispered into its mysterious interiors, "I'm not the biggest whale. There are bigger whales than me." Suddenly he had changed the exigencies of the ocean into the dangers of the street. "You don't bother us and we won't bother you. Go back where you came from. We don't want to harm you," and each day he returned to the saga and embellished it. Thanks to the dedicated cadre of poet-teachers at work in the United States who have learned what the power of poetry means, all across America the children are singing! The little boy madly waves his hand at me, "I'm a poetry too," and a first grade girl tucks this line into her poem, "Do you believe in me? If you don't I won't be free." The thank-you note from a third grader from the Boston city schools says, "I will think of you in the place where good thoughts are remembered."

I have learned so much from the children, and from the teachers who have embraced the poetry process once they begin to understand that they have a place in it too, the teachers who have found ways to weave poetry into the everyday life of the classroom and find their classroom a happier and healthier place to dwell because of it. It is you: children, parents, and teachers: all practitioners of the lively art of poem-making, whom we thank, honor and greet in the third printing of *Beyond Words*.

Elizabeth McKim